Three Score Years ... and Then?

A study of the nutrition and wellbeing of elderly people at home

Louise Davies, PHD, FAHE

Head, Gerontology Nutrition Unit,
Queen Elizabeth College,
University of London.

William Heinemann Medical Books Limited · London

William Heinemann Medical Books Limited
23 Bedford Square
London WC1B 3HH

First published 1981

Copyright © Louise Davies 1981

ISBN 0 433 07193 1

Printed and bound in Great Britain by
Robert Hartnoll Limited,
Bodmin, Cornwall

Composition in Garamond by
Filmtype Services Limited
Scarborough, North Yorkshire

THREE SCORE YEARS ... AND THEN?

Dedication

for

Professor Arnold E. Bender
Kate Hastrop
Dr M. Diane Holdsworth

without whom this book could not have been written.

Contents

Foreword

Until thirty years ago there was little scientific interest in the medical, social, psychological and nutritional problems of the elderly in our population. One of the earliest studies of the elderly living at home was that carried out in Sheffield in 1953 and in this survey nutritional data as well as social, medical and biochemical data were collected. Dr Louise Davies is herself one of the pioneers of some of the early studies and in 1968 she established the Gerontology Nutrition Unit at Queen Elizabeth College, London, with the aim of bridging the gap between nutritional research and its practical applications.

In the years 1967 and 1968 the first large scale national study of the nutritional status of the elderly population was conducted by geriatric physicians in collaboration with nutritionists. This study was instigated by the Committee on Medical and Nutritional Aspects of Food Policy, an organisation set up by the Government during World War II, because it was thought that the special medical, social and economic problems of the elderly might place them in a position of particular risk. Since then numerous reports of different aspects of the relationships between nutrition and health in old age have been published. More is now known about the nutritional status of the elderly in the British Isles than for any other country in the world and there is also a considerable body of knowledge of the risk factors in the older individual's pattern of living which are conducive to malnutrition. Thus we now have the information on which to formulate policy, but there still remains a gap between the data revealed by the numerous reports and the practical steps which must be taken to improve the nutritional status of the older members of the population.

I feel greatly honoured by being invited to write these words of introduction since this book represents a pioneer effort to translate increasing knowledge in this hitherto neglected field into sound nutritional policy by an author who is herself both a nutritionist and an educationist.

Professor A.N. Exton-Smith CBE, MD, FRCP
Barlow Professor of Geriatric Medicine
Faculty of Clinical Sciences
University College London

Preface

The Gerontology Nutrition Unit* has looked at the nutrition of a diversity of older people in the United Kingdom. The particular study described in this book examined the nutrition of those already considered to be at nutritional and perhaps also social risk, and therefore receiving meals-on-wheels. As there was a pattern of two meals-on-wheels a week being delivered to over half the recipients in the UK at this period (1970), arrangements were made to conduct a survey in a district providing this number of delivered meals.

An investigation was to be made of the delivered meals *together with their value in the total diet*. Thus it was not to be just a narrow 'meals-on-wheels survey'; instead a picture would be built up of the general nutrition of a group of elderly people.

The scope expanded still further because we included detailed questionnaires on socio-economic background. Our findings then seemed to point not only to problems, but also to possible solutions. The practicability of some of these solutions was put to the test before the writing of this book.

For whom is the book intended? Primarily for those in the social services (including administrators) concerned with the care of an elderly generation; also geriatricians and other medical practitioners; nutritionists and dietitians; students, including those studying nutrition, home economics, medicine, sociology, social work, and social history; and anyone connected with elderly men or women through voluntary work or family commitments.

Because of this range of readership, I have deliberately steered a wide course, areas of which can be taken at speed by some, and explored in depth by others. The text includes basic nutrition, simple explanations and background information, as well as (largely in the Appendix) the tables and the data essential for serious study.

Louise Davies   *London 1981*

---

*The Gerontology Nutrition Unit was established in 1968 by the author to bridge the gap between basic nutritional research and its practical applications for elderly men and women, and those caring for them. The Unit, in the Nutrition Department of Queen Elizabeth College, London University, is independently financed by grants and charitable donations.

Acknowledgements

The views expressed in this book are not necessarily those of the many friends and colleagues to whom I turned for advice. My thanks to all of them, and in particular the following:

AT QUEEN ELIZABETH COLLEGE: Professor Arnold E. Bender, Dr M. Diane Holdsworth, the late Dr G.W. Lynch, Mr Brian Meek, Mr Derek Miller, Dr R.H.J. Watson, and Professor John Yudkin.

FOR COMMENT: Professor Sir W. Ferguson Anderson, Professor R.D. Cohen, Mrs M. Disselduff, Dr Wilfred Harding, Dr R.E. Hughes, and Mrs Freda Patton.

IN PORTSMOUTH co-operation was received from: Mr Reg Humphries, previously Director of Social Services, City of Portsmouth; numerous members of staff of Social Services and Health Services; Dr P.G. Roads, former Medical Officer, Portsmouth, the Public Analyst and Scientific Adviser for the City of Portsmouth, and his assistant, Mrs Audrey Pearce; The WRVS Organiser and volunteers on the meals-on-wheels rounds; Mrs Lodge, Kitchen Supervisor, and the meals-on-wheels kitchen staff.

Special thanks are due to Mrs Kate Hastrop and her team of interviewers: Mrs Betty Wintle, Mrs Jane Harris and Mrs Barbara Lock; and of course to the 100 men and women who agreed to take part in the survey.

My particular thanks go to Scoular Anderson for drawing the cartoons, thereby helping me to retain a sense of humour.

The work of the Gerontology Nutrition Unit has been generously sponsored by:

Flour Advisory Bureau	National Dairy Council	Sainsbury Charitable Fund
Marks and Spencer Ltd	Neville Williams Trust	Unilever Ltd
Milk Marketing Board	Potato Marketing Board	United Biscuits Ltd

Donations have been received over the years from:

Bovril Ltd; British Gas; Cadbury – Schweppes Foods Ltd; Community Relations Commission; The Electrical Association for Women; H.J. Heinz & Co., Ltd; Horlicks Charitable Trust; John Lewis Partnership; Metal Box Co; Nestlé Company; Peel Medical Research Fund; Spillers Ltd.

The main sponsors of our current research are the National Dairy Council, through an award made by the EEC.

Notes on units

In common with all in the biological and medical sciences, nutritionists now use the internationally accepted SI system of units. Thus energy is measured in joules*, and amounts of substances such as potassium in *millimoles* (mmol).

At the time when the survey described in this book was conducted, however, 'old' metric units were still in use, and the even older *ounces* were used in the measurement of food portions, as they were more familiar to the subjects and better suited to home weighing.

Thus a mixture of units is used in this book. Those accustomed to SI units will be able to make the appropriate conversions from conversion figures given in the text. For many readers it is anticipated that the older units, particularly the ounce and the nutritional *calorie* (kcal), will be more familiar.

A WHO manual, *The SI for the Health Professions*, notes:
> The principal obstacle to the use of the joule alone in nutrition is the fact that dietary tables giving values in joules are not yet widely available. As an interim measure, therefore, it is preferable that values be quoted in both joules and calories . . .

Where food prices were originally recorded in 'old' currency, conversion into decimal values has not been attempted, as comparison with present-day prices could only be misleading.

---

*1 kcal = 4.2 kilojoules (kJ)   1000 kJ = 1 megajoule (MJ)

1
Attitudes to old age

Too often, in our attitudes to old age, we treat the elderly as a group, not as individuals. 'They', we say, eat less as they grow older. 'They', we say, are set in their ways and will not try new foods. 'They' lose their sense of taste; 'they' need soft foods because they cannot chew; 'they' are poverty stricken and cannot afford a normal nourishing diet at today's prices. In other words, too often we approach the nutrition — and the malnutrition — of the elderly as (to use the present day jargon) a 'group situation'.

The results of this group summing up can be highly detrimental to the very individuals we are trying to help. For instance, why should we assume that 'they' eat less as they grow older? Loss of appetite, with subsequent loss of weight, may be a symptom of illness or distress, not 'just old age'. These are symptoms to be investigated, with a view to possible treatment.

Moreover, group summing up can produce group solutions which many elderly individuals do not need and, just as important, do not want. For example, do you really believe that most elderly individuals would prefer special so-called 'geriatric foods' to familiar home cooking? Yet special foods are often suggested, not just for a few on special diets, but for 'the elderly'.

'Group think' has led some people to take it for granted that when elderly people are at nutritional risk they are *either* clients for meals-on-wheels, *or* capable of going to luncheon clubs; like the Gilbert and Sullivan ditty:

> That every boy and every gal
> That's born into this world alive
> Is either a little Liberal
> Or else a little Conservative

However, a combination of meals-on-wheels and luncheon clubs can be even more valuable than either taken separately.

'Group think' has led, in a number of districts, to the aim of delivering at least 5 meals-on-wheels a week to most recipients, ideally raising this to 7 a week. But what are the needs and the wishes of the recipients themselves? This was one of the questions which we posed in the survey which is described in this book. The answer to the question may come as a surprise to the planners, and the full implications of our findings are explored in depth.

Before we can assume that at present we are providing answers to nutritional needs we need to ask many more questions. In the words of J.C. McKenzie, a Research Sociologist:

> One of the remarkable things about nutrition is that in the area between chronic deficiency and optimum health, more is known about animals than about man. Thus in animal nutrition a clear distinction is drawn between minimum requirements for health, under which no specific symptoms of deficiency occur, and 'optimum-nutrition' where a maximum growth occurs. No study designed to examine whether a similar concept is valid for humans has been undertaken. Indeed it is difficult to assess whether such a study would be realistic because one of the major difficulties is to decide what we mean by 'optimum' health for humans. Does it mean maximum growth, maximum resistance to disease, long life, or what? For animals the issue is usually more clear cut — they are fed for maximum growth, maximum milk yield or some other specific criterion.

In humans, a desirable criterion is often taken to be 'long life'. Those who have attained their 100th birthday are interviewed. To the inevitable question 'to what do you attribute your long life?' I heard one centenarian on Canadian TV reply with disarming honesty 'I really don't know; if I'd known I was going to live this long, I'd have taken more care of myself!'

But most centenarians are absolutely certain — and completely divided — on the reason for survival: 'yogurt and honey' . . . 'good plain food'; 'taking things steady' . . . 'exercise in all weathers'; 'I've been a bachelor and always independent' . . . 'the loving care of my beloved wife'. This diversity of answers can be summed up in the story of the centenarian whose reply to the question was: 'I've reached a hundred years because I've never smoked, I don't touch alcohol and I don't go with women'. The interview was interrupted by a sudden crashing sound from next door. 'Take no notice' said the old man, 'it's just my father. He always quarrels with his fancy woman when he's drunk because she nags him about his smoking!'

There are other criteria, evidenced in the answers to another perennial question: 'What do you want most in life?' Again, the answers vary: health; happiness; wealth; a contented family life; social involvement; independence; fame ... Surely the criterion we should be looking for is not the number of years, but — for each individual — the quality of those years.

This book is focusing on the nutrition of over 9 million Retirement Pensioners in the United Kingdom, but I am deliberately narrowing the field so that the people we are describing represent some of those who are already considered to be most in nutritional and social need. They are among the 2½–3% of the elderly population already in receipt of meals-on-wheels.

However, the field needs to be narrowed even further: we have to look at the problems not merely of a group, but of individuals. *By studying the nutritional problems of the 100 individuals described in this book we can learn a great deal about the potential problems of the 9 million.*

It would be fascinating to see what we could learn also from studying the complete opposite of these meals-on-wheels recipients: those members of the community who have survived to a vigorous old age. They have been called 'the elderly élite'. Could it not be that health in old age is the norm? Are we right in explaining away long years of debilitating disorders as 'just old age'. It strikes me as a defeatest attitude that we are not unduly shocked when old age is treated as a time of illness, accident, depression, obstinacy or apathy. Old people complain 'My joints are full of aches and pains' and we say, 'Of course — they are getting old'.

I am not yet classified as elderly, so if I get aches and pains I go to the doctor because it isn't 'right' at my age. Why should it be 'right' later on? Alex Comfort tells the story of the man of 104 who, when he complained of a painful stiff right knee was told 'After all, you can't expect to be agile' and replied, 'My left knee's 104 too, and that doesn't hurt!'

Why do we look at lively, healthy elderly people and say 'Aren't they wonderful'? It would be a better incentive to research to think on the words of the 19th century cleric and essayist, the Reverend Sydney Smith, who once jested of such a man 'He is remarkably well, considering that he has been remarkably well for so many years!' It is an unsolved puzzle: what has kept them 'remarkably well'?

The importance of the role of diet in preventive medicine (i.e. the effect of food intake on health) is becoming increasingly recognised.

Heart attacks are now being blamed, amongst other things, on too much animal fat or too much sugar in the diet. The possible role of dietary fibre in the prevention of diseases is much under discussion. Blindness due to cataracts, shakiness in the elderly, and other conditions that lead to the hazard of falls, could be caused by nutritional disorders. Poor nutrition contributes to the pains of joints and muscles; osteomalacia is an example.

The opposite phenomenon (the effect of health on food intake) is already recognised: serious ill-health can markedly affect appetite. For example, chronic bronchitis can be responsible for anorexia; patients suffering from small but repeated cerebral accidents are generally confused, and patients who have suffered these strokes may have difficulty in eating and swallowing.

Sometimes a prescribed drug can set in motion other ailments. It is recognised that drugs, or combinations of drugs, can impair the absorption of nutrients. So too can over-consumption of alcohol, including excessive use of 'tonic wine'. The interaction of drugs and nutrients is a large subject, but to take just two examples, the antibiotic tetracycline may impair iron absorption in those already anaemic, and oral diuretics cause excessive loss of potassium along with the fluid excretion, and this potassium needs to be replaced.

So we have seen that lack or excess of a specific nutrient may be a contributing factor to diseases, including some at present attributed to 'just old age'; some diseases – including those particularly prevalent in the elderly – affect nutrient intake; some drugs, used in the control of diseases, impair nutritional status. There is, furthermore, a serious sociological effect to be considered. A long history of pain or illness can sometimes lead to a pessimistic and demanding attitude to life in later years, or else to extreme variability in mood; these off-putting attitudes frequently drive the family to despair, guilt or frustration to the point of distraction, and thus can rebound miserably upon those needing, and longing for, extra care and attention.

I am *not* saying that better nutrition will automatically cure most diseases or postpone death. As Dr Samuel Johnson announced: 'My diseases are an asthma, a dropsy and, what is less curable, 75'. Yet already some people (generally those becoming old) hope science will find a way of prolonging the life span; they are actually asking us to prolong the period when so many are unfit and unhealthy. Others (sometimes those who are young) even recommend euthanasia at the age of 70. Euthanasia, or a longer life span — which? This is like offering a prisoner the choice between capital punishment and life imprisonment.

To sum up, what I am saying is that the elderly are not just a section of the population, they are a cross-section. They are individuals, and many of them have nutritional problems which call for individual solutions. Well-meaning group solutions may even do harm.

The quantity of years is being increased for many who would in previous generations have died young. But we have not yet adequately recognised and applied the preventive measures which could improve the *quality* of those years. It is at this point that we should begin to define nutrition in its broader sense, and to emphasise that the term malnourishment can cover deprivation in spheres other than foods and physical health. Inextricably linked together are social, economic, emotional and environmental malnourishment and this book will be examining all these aspects.

2
Some landmarks in the study of the nutrition of the elderly in the UK

In the past, one generally had the survival of the fittest. Nowadays, the advancement of Science is helping more old people to survive; but many of them are neither at their fittest, nor at their happiest. Good nutrition, particularly in the broader sense mentioned at the end of the previous chapter, could have a marked effect on their health, happiness and independence. This is important personally to the individual; politically to a Welfare State.

The number of elderly people has strikingly increased, mainly it is claimed, because of improvements in sanitation and nutrition, and because with medical advances there has been a fall in the death rate at younger ages. At the 1901 Census there were fewer than 2½ million elderly men and women in the United Kingdom (6·2% of the total population). By 1971 there were 9 million 'persons of pensionable age' in the UK (16·2% of the total population). These 1971 figures are from the Census nearest to the time of the meals-on-wheels survey reported in this book. This high proportion — and especially the increasing numbers of the over 80s — has helped to lead to present day concern with the health and nutrition problems of 'the elderly', the term applied — though I and many others would dispute it — to women 60 years and over and men 65 years and over, i.e. 'persons of pensionable age'.

By the beginning of this century there was already concern with the social and economic aspects of old age. A non-contributory Old Age Pension was introduced in the 1908 Budget of the then Chancellor of the Exchequer, Mr Asquith; soon afterwards, when Asquith became Prime Minister, it was carried through by his successor, Lloyd George. It allowed payment of 5 shillings per week to elderly persons (men or women over 70 years of age) with an income of under £31 per annum. The original Bill contained provision to exclude anyone who had been in prison or on Poor Relief in the last 20 years, and also to deprive pensioners of the vote; but these clauses were struck out before it became law.

But there were many misgivings that such pensions could only tend to encourage the thriftless; sentiments reminiscent of some present-day attitudes to student grants and social security payments! Peter Wilsher (1970) quotes a report by the *Woman Worker*, a crusading weekly, which pointed out to a disapproving Lord Provost of Glasgow how one 'typically thriftless' elderly Glasgow widow intended to spend her 5s 0d.: Rent: 2s 3d; pint of paraffin 1½d; 14 lb coal 2½d; 2 oz tea 1d; ½ lb sugar 1½d; 2 lb potatoes 1d; 2 lb loin of mutton 1s 0d; half-bag of flour 1d; pint of porter (for Sunday's dinner) 1¾d; pepper, salt and vinegar 1½d; one loaf 2½d. This made a total of 4s 5¼d. The old lady said she intended to have a first-class dinner on Sunday, with perhaps a pennyworth of cheese. Later in the week she would purchase 'a ha'porth of beans' together with 'a penn'orth of onions', and after that she calculated she would have enough left over to afford 1d for a herring on Friday, 'and then it will be time for me to draw my pension again.'

In January 1909 the first payments were made, and Wilsher describes bonfires and scenes of great rejoicing. In Walworth, one old woman offered the Postmaster two rashers of bacon for helping her to fill up the forms. Similarly *Lark Rise to Candleford* by Flora Thompson shows how life was transformed for aged cottagers who had been in daily fear of the workhouse. 'There were flowers from their gardens and apples from their trees for the girl who merely handed them the money.'

The Contributory Old Age Pension was introduced in 1925. The emphasis was still on the social and economic problems of old age; indeed one would not expect to find any nutritional surveys of the elderly at that date because the science of nutrition was an almost unknown subject. However, even a general study of geriatrics lagged far behind the already advanced study of paediatrics and the first Professor of Geriatric Medicine in the UK, W. Ferguson Anderson of Glasgow, was not appointed until 1965. In a book published two years later he stressed the importance of preventive medicine and the practical steps which can help with the medical, social and psychological problems of the elderly. In 1971, in the second edition of his book, a new chapter was added on the nutrition of the elderly. In a modern day textbook on geriatric medicine, it was taken for granted that a chapter on nutrition should be included (Davies 1981).

At present, although there are fewer than 15 Chairs of Geriatric Medicine in the UK, there is continuous pressure to encourage special help, nutritional as well as social, for the elderly.

Conversely the American Medical Association had made a policy decision not to isolate geriatrics as a medical speciality, nor to encourage the setting up of special facilities for the care of the elderly. They believe it important to integrate the elderly into the rest of the community (Watkin, 1968a). However some elderly Americans themselves do not want integration with the rest of the community. They have established 'Sunshine Cities' with all the inhabitants in the older age brackets; younger friends or relations who visit must leave them in peace, quit the town and stay out of bounds by evening. American 'Gray Panthers' are the greying militants who feel that the elderly not only have much wisdom to offer the young, but are also capable of devising their own well-being. That special problems of the elderly exist, however, was shown by the calling of the White House Conference on Aging (1971); its reports included one on Nutrition.

SURVEYS IN THE UNITED KINGDOM

There have so far been few surveys of health and nutrition of the elderly in the UK, and some of these have examined only particular nutrients. There is very little information linking social and economic factors with the health and nutrition of elderly people. It has been rightly said that few if any socio-economic studies have included evidence that the nutritionist would regard as adequate; the reverse is also true.

It seems incredible that as recently as 1953 a survey conducted in Sheffield (Bransby and Osborne) on 303 elderly subjects was able to claim: 'The present survey provides *for the first time* data on food consumption and the intake of calories and nutrients for a reasonably large group of elderly persons living alone' (my italics). In their survey, records could be obtained from more people up to 74 years than those 75 years and over. Many more of the subjects were living with a spouse than were living alone; but the survey found that generally those living alone ate less of the foods requiring preparation than did the married couples. The authors stated, 'it is not possible to say whether the nutrient intakes of the groups studied were satisfactory or not, simply because there are so few data for the elderly'.

Commenting on this lack of data, other investigators concerned with the survey (Hobson *et al.*, 1955) suggested that the intakes of the fit group in the survey and the intakes of a small group in residential homes might provide a working basis for estimating the nutrient intakes of the elderly. In the diet study it had been found that a substantial proportion of the subjects, especially the women, were eating less food than required to supply the energy and nutrients recommended by the British Medical Association (1950) for 'adults with sedentary work and little travelling.' It is interesting that although the DHSS Recommended Intakes of Nutrients for the UK (1969) had special categories for elderly men and elderly women, their recommendations show little change from the 1950 figures for calorie (kcal) intakes (*1950*: Women 2000 kcal; Men 2250 kcal. *1969*: Elderly Women 1900–2050 kcal; Elderly Men 2100–2350 kcal). (For the latest Recommended Daily Amounts (1979), see page 52.)

Due to the lack of data and survey material, advice on diet in old age could be as vague as 'in old age one should eat sparingly; the food should be easily chewed and bulky food avoided' (Hutchison 1934).

This theme was continued during the next decade:

> The danger of overfeeding the old is almost as great as that of underfeeding the young; an excess of nourishment chokes instead of feeding the flickering flame of life. Leanness and longevity go together, and a man will only roll all the faster down the hill of life if his figure be rotund

(Hutchison and Mottram in the edition of 1936; repeated in the edition of 1948). But before we smile too broadly at this, it is noteworthy that most of the recent experimental work on obesity points to the same conclusions!

In less general terms, interest in problems of the elderly was being aroused. In 1948 Dr J.H. Sheldon was already drawing attention to a marked increase of infirmity and disability after the age of 75 years. In a random sample of old people in Wolverhampton, 32% of those over 85 years of age were housebound.

In 1960 Dr Suzanne M. Lempert, of the Department of Social and Preventive Medicine at the University of Manchester, described the Stockport Survey of the Aged in which about 2100 men and women over the age of 80 years were interviewed. Nutritional data were limited but there was a rough classification of diet by counting the number of hot meals eaten; the diets of a small sample of those interviewed were studied more fully. It was reported that 'about half of the subjects did not eat a hot balanced meal every day. Old people living alone often had an inadequate diet'. (But one wonders what criteria were used to define 'balanced meal' and 'inadequate diet'.) The report on these over 80s continued 'the best fed were those cared for by the younger generation, those of high social class, independent means, and especially those who continued to work. Over two thirds of the women still did some cooking, many without help, but the meals prepared were not always adequate'. Widowers had the poorest diets. 'Marriage keeps particularly the old men healthy'. Luncheon clubs were said to provide important supplements. The survey was later described fully in a book (Brockington and Lempert, 1966).

Thus by the 1960s we are beginning to find more correlation between age, social circumstances and diet patterns (Townsend and Wedderburn, 1965). More emphasis was being placed on the needs of the elderly. Dr John Maddison, Area Medical Officer for Teddington, Middlesex,was strongly advocating preventive medicine for older people, and succeeded in setting up an experimental clinic in Teddington. In 1963 he wrote a Report in which he showed that he had diagnosed many defects, including malnutrition, in patients who might not otherwise have seen a doctor. Despite lack of controls, because multiple treatments were given, Dr Maddison reported success from the introduction of 'preventive medicine'.

Miss Amelia Harris, of the Government Social Survey, was asked to carry out an enquiry (1968) into the Social Welfare of the Elderly on behalf of the National Corporation for the Care of Old People and the Scottish Home and Health Department. It was a study in 13 local authority areas in England, Wales and Scotland. Miss Harris had, in December 1959, produced the results of an enquiry into the meals-on-wheels services and this will be referred to in Chapter 4. But in her enquiries, which gave much valuable information to the planners, the nutritive value of the meals was not considered.

The King Edward's Hospital Fund publication of a *Report of an Investigation into the Dietary of Elderly Women Living Alone* (Exton-Smith and Stanton, 1965) represented a landmark in dietary surveys of the elderly. It was encouraging that the findings for the whole group of 60 elderly women did not bear out the popular idea that many old people who live alone exist almost entirely on bread, butter, jam, biscuits and cups of sweetened tea.

> In the main, subjects ate a varied diet, cooked at least one meal a day and frequently ate fruit and vegetables. That is not to say that *all* had an excellent diet as was shown by the wide range of intakes.

The authors, however, recognised limitations of this survey: they excluded men, women on special diets, and those who were too deaf for easy communication or too confused to understand.

> It may well be that the least satisfactorily nourished people were not included . . . because the techniques followed demanded too high a degree of co-operation and understanding for the mentally confused or lethargic. Yet it is these very people who are likely to be poorly nourished.

Recognising the limitations of cross-sectional* studies with the elderly, Stanton and Exton-Smith (1970) carried out a longitudinal† study on 22 of the original subjects (16 of these with a week's weighed survey). Among their conclusions was that there was a group of individuals whose nutrient intakes changed little with age. These subjects are the fortunate élite (to whom we have already drawn attention in the first chapter) who reach extreme old age with little impairment in their health and physical capabilities. Reference is made to Watkin (1968b) who points out that it has not yet been determined whether their life-long nutrition pattern has contributed to their longevity; or whether their heredity has not only enabled them to survive but has also, in some manner, characterised their nutrition.

The King Edward's Hospital Fund Report of 1965 had seemingly aroused latent interests in the nutrition of the elderly. The problems and research findings were of interest to the community at large as well as to Government and voluntary bodies (such as Help the Aged and the National Old People's Welfare Council — later to be known as Age Concern).

---

*cross-sectional study: a single study. Findings in 70-year-olds would be compared with those in 80-year-olds at the same time.
†longitudinal study: a follow-up study some time later, on the same subjects to compare the later with the earlier results, i.e. those in a first study at 70 years would be those aged 80 in a second, longitudinal study ten years later.

In 1967 the Camberwell Nutritional Survey (Bhaskar Rao and Kataria) studied the dietary habits, socio-economic background and clinical nutritional state of 129 elderly people. They stressed that the scope of their study was rather limited and did not expect to arrive at any spectacular results. They, too, found nutritional surveys of the elderly particularly time-consuming, with accurate information difficult to elicit and needing careful assessment. Nevertheless, they said, there is continuing need for such surveys.

It was at about this time that I made the suggestion that the elderly should be included, with other nutritionally vulnerable groups, in the Welfare Food Services (Bender and Davies, 1968). But this was not to be — later even the milk-in-schools service was severely curtailed. However, maybe the time will one day be politically ripe for some re-thinking on behalf of the elderly.

Aware of the nutritional vulnerability of the elderly, in 1968 I established the Geriatric Nutrition Unit (later, as its scope widened, re-named the Gerontology Nutrition Unit) at Queen Elizabeth College, London University. Its aim was to bridge the gap between nutritional research and practical applications. This approach aroused interest not only in the UK but also abroad.

In 1972 a Nutrition Survey of the Elderly (DHSS) reported on 879 men and women aged 65 and over in six areas of England and Scotland. The data had been gathered in 1967/8. *This was the first large scale government enquiry into the nutritional status of the elderly.* The clinicians found:

> some but not much overt malnutrition ... the most important reason for malnutrition when it occurred was often an under-lying medical condition rather than a poor diet. Nevertheless the survey does show that some old people — even though they may have been only a very small proportion of a sample which included a high proportion of those at special risk — were demonstrably malnourished. There were others for whom more could have been done and others still whose margin of safety must have been narrow. We are certainly not justified in concluding that present services give all the assistance which is required.

It is of interest that, when the clinicians in the different areas were investigating forms of mild malnutrition in the elderly,

> there were substantial differences in the nature and amount of malnutrition diagnosed in the various areas, partly reflecting the special interests of each clinician, partly the severity of his criteria of malnutrition.

The difficulties of relating clinical and biochemical findings to nutritional deficiencies alone are well recognised. Moreover the position is complicated by the fact that malnutrition in the elderly is often multifactorial in origin. These difficulties were stressed again in a follow-up Report 5 years later on 365 of the original subjects (DHSS, 1979).

Despite these problems, the importance of nutritional research has been recognised particularly on groups of the elderly population considered most at risk. For instance, in a report of the proceedings of a symposium, *Vitamins in the Elderly* (Exton-Smith and Scott, 1968) attention was drawn to low intakes of vitamin C, folate, B_{12}, thiamin and riboflavin. There have been nutritional investigations conducted on geriatric patients in hospital (e.g. Evans and Stock, 1971; 1972), the housebound (Exton-Smith *et al.*, 1972), residents in old people's homes (Davies and Holdsworth, 1979), elderly men and women in Edinburgh (Lonergan, 1971), the elderly at home (Macleod *et al.*, 1974), the institutionalised in Northern Ireland (Vir and Love, 1979) and people receiving luncheon club meals or meals-on-wheels (Stanton, 1971; Davies *et al.*, 1973–75; Scottish Health Service Studies No. 35; Local Authority Reports, e.g. Bedfordshire, Camden, Harrow, Havering, Hillingdon, Kingston-upon-Thames, Nottingham, South Glamorgan, Worcestershire).

It is unfortunate that these Local Authority reports and others which are now being written, are often limited in circulation. They can be unknown to those outside the specific area; there is a danger that their findings may be duplicated instead of being compared and shared.

3
The elderly in the community

The emphasis in the UK is to keep elderly men and women active and independent as long as possible; during the period of our survey, fewer than 3% of the total elderly population were in residential homes; fewer than 3% in hospitals. Over 70% (as shown later in this chapter) were in 'one or two person households'. Others were living with their families, or in sheltered housing or other accommodation, still within the community. But many of these in the community are admittedly ill, demanding or dependent.

Three kinds of organisation provide services:

1 Central Government Departments, e.g. DHSS.
2 Local Government Departments
3 Voluntary, e.g. Age Concern, Help the Aged, the Centre for Policy on Ageing (formerly the National Corporation for the Care of Old People), WRVS, Red Cross, numerous local organisations and charities (funds from the general public, sometimes with Government or Local Authority help).

Many of the services provided, particularly most of the facilities of the National Health Service (NHS), are free for all residents in the UK regardless of age. Others, such as housing aids and adaptations and subsidized meals-on-wheels, are given, once a need is established, to the disabled or chronic sick of any age. To encourage GPs to take on or keep elderly patients, the State pays the doctor a higher *per capita* fee (although not all elderly people need or get the advantage of this in home visits or more of the doctor's time and attention).

Within the NHS, geriatric medicine has developed as a speciality, involving the growth of separate departments with consultant and junior medical staff. This has many advantages, but it can be argued that it may be against the best interests of elderly people, who, because of limited medical resources, may be deprived of some of the wider skilled service, social care and hospital accommodation given to younger people. Recently there has been some reorientation towards closer association with general medicine.

Some of the services listed below are available to all 'persons of pensionable age'; others are allocated according to priority needs or financial circumstances and their availability may vary from one local authority to another. They may include help with:

Income — retirement pensions, supplementary pensions, exceptional circumstances additions (e.g. for special diets). Individuals may also have an income from a second pension (from employer's or private scheme), savings and investments, or from charitable grants.

Health — General practitioner, hospital or surgery under the NHS, geriatric hospitals including day hospitals, free prescriptions and appliances, chiropody, hearing aids and (if in receipt of Supplementary Benefit) free dental treatment and spectacles.

Housing — aids and adaptations, in some cases free heaters, house insulation and help with heating bills, help to obtain special housing (e.g. one bedroom bungalows, flats, warden supervised flats, sheltered housing), sometimes rent and rate rebates.

Independence at Home — visits from health visitors, social workers, home nurse, home help (mainly for cleaning, shopping and sometimes food preparation or cooking), meals-on-wheels and luncheon clubs, day centres, clubs (general, social or specialised, e.g. for the deaf or hard of hearing), laundry services, Good Neighbour or young people's Task Force services, such as visiting, shopping, sharing of meals or snacks, redecorating, gardening, library book changing, writing letters.

Residential Homes for the Elderly — generally small communities, not offering long-term nursing — Local Authority, voluntary (non-profit making) or private (commercial).

Work and Leisure — part-time work, over 60s employment agencies, new careers, sheltered workshops, hobbies, further education (including over 60s or Retirement Cookery Classes), social outings, (including 'Contact' organised tea parties), holidays for the elderly at reduced rates or free, in some districts bus passes and concessionary fares on rail and underground, reduced rate museums, cinemas and theatres, hairdressing and also — of paramount importance — helping others.

Of particular help to the frail: television, radio, talking books, newsletters, large print books, mobile libraries. But the cost of installation and rental of a telephone may prove prohibitive.

In spite of all these services, a review of the conditions of the elderly in Britain today gives many indications that this elderly age group includes more seriously disadvantaged people than does any other (Jefferys, 1976).

PUBLIC EXPENDITURE

It is difficult to obtain a breakdown of public expenditure in terms of 'Health and Welfare' but the following figures give 'The estimated Total Public Expenditure on Persons of Pensionable Age'.

	Social Security £m	Health and Welfare £m	Total £m
1963–64	1119	303	1422
1971–72	2499	722	3221

Much of this increase reflects inflation of costs and prices as well as the increase in numbers of the elderly. The increase in expenditure at constant prices was about 25%.

The proportion of the Gross National Product spent on services to the elderly in 1978 was 9·33%.

POPULATION FIGURES

Increase in Numbers of Persons of Pensionable Age (women 60 and over, men 65 and over) in the UK

Home Population (Census Figures)

1901		2·4 million (6·2% of total population)
1911		2·9 million
1921	[1]	3·6 million
1931	[1]	4·4 million
1941	no census due to the war
1951		6·8 million
1961		7·7 million
1968	[2]	8·6 million
1971		9·0 million (16·2% of total population)

[1] Figures included for Northern Ireland are estimated
[2] Mid-year estimate of the home population

Circumstances

Persons over pensionable age (1971 Census, Great Britain) in:

One person households	24·2%	(2 133 050)
Two person households	48·1%	(4 238 165)
Other households	22·5%	(1 986 160)
NHS hospitals	2·2%	(192 360)
Other hospitals	0·3%	(24 940)
Other establishments	2·6%	(233 250)

Single, widowed or divorced (1971 Census, UK):

82% of women aged 75 & over
43% of men aged 75 & over

In employment:

Aged 60–64: 80% of men and 25–30% of women

After 65 years of age the proportion at work, already falling, drops rapidly. The 1971 census is based on confidential returns and may under-estimate the amount of part-time work done:

65 years and over, in employment: 19% of men and 6% of women

The 'Older Elderly'

Ratio of women to men (1971 Census, UK):

AGE 80   AGE 85

Aged 80   2:1   Aged 85   2·5:1

Population aged 80 and over (UK):

1971 Census   1·3 million

Total population projection (based on a UK mid-1976 estimate):

2000 (mid-1976 projection)   2·0 million

Centenarians in the UK

In 1977 the Secretary of State for Social Services sent 1100 congratulatory telegrams to Retirement Pensioners celebrating their 100th birthday (figures from DHSS); 930 of these telegrams were sent to women, 170 to men. Her Majesty the Queen also sends telegrams to her subjects on their 100th birthday.

The population projectionists forecast a continual growth in the British population aged 65 and over, but at a diminishing rate (Government Actuaries Department 1975). If their predictions are correct (and they are better for obvious reasons in forecasting total numbers of elderly in the next three decades than they are the total numbers of newborn), the total numbers in the age bracket 65–74 will increase only slightly between 1971 and 1991 (i.e., by less than 1%) but there will be an increase of over a third in the numbers aged 75–84 and of nearly a half (46·24%) in those aged 85 and over. Moreover, if there is any reduction in the mortality rate of middle aged men, and there is ample room for such an improvement, the increase will be even greater (Jefferys 1976).

Numbers Receiving Meals-on-Wheels and Luncheon Club Meals

In the survey described in this book, all the 100 elderly men and women studied in Portsmouth were receiving two meals-on-wheels per week, and some were attending luncheon clubs. Nationwide figures for these services are given below.

Approximately 1½–2% of the total elderly population of the UK received meals-on-wheels at the time of our survey in 1970. By 1979 this figure had risen to approximately 2½–3%.

The advantage of meals-on-wheels is that 'the meal is taken to the diner', but this can also bring disadvantages. It not only causes a time-lag between cooking and consumption, but also means the recipient stays at home. Some who receive meals-on-wheels are entirely housebound, but others would welcome a change of scene and company (especially if transport could be provided). Incidentally, the vast majority of meals-on-wheels recipients are over 65 years of age; less than 2% are in younger age groups.

It can be seen from Table 1 that the total number of meals-on-wheels delivered in England has nearly doubled in less than a decade, from just over 14 million in 1970 to more than 26 million by 1978/9 (figures for Wales, Scotland and Northern Ireland are calculated separately). However the main expansion took place by

Table 1
Deliveries of meals-on-wheels in England
(DHSS Local Authority Statistics)

| | **Number of meals served (millions)** | | | | |
	1970	1971/2	1974/5	1976/7	1978/9
Meals served at home	14·2	15·8	23·5	24·6	26·2
Served by:					
WRVS	6·8 (47·7%)				9·6 (36·6%)
Local Authority	4·9 (34·6%)				13·8 (52·8%)
Other voluntary organisations	2·5 (17·7%)				2·8 (10·6%)
Meals served elsewhere (luncheon clubs, etc.)	7·4	8·9	14·4	16·6	14·8*

*The decrease in numbers of club meals in 1978/9 is because figures now exclude those meals which are taken at a centre while the recipient is attending for some other purpose such as occupational therapy.

1974, since when the increase in numbers served has been more gradual.

The large increase in the numbers served has been mainly due to the expansion in the Local Authority service. Even with this expansion, there are still elderly people on waiting lists for meals-on-wheels. There are many others who cannot even be considered for a waiting list because the local meals-on-wheels facilities are already over-stretched.

Table 2
Deliveries of meals-on-wheels in a Sample Week (England)

	1970	1978/9
Total number meals-on-wheels served	304 035	550 887
Number of persons in receipt of meals-on-wheels	112 369	178 826
Number of persons receiving 1 meal	11 416 (10·2%)	12 880 (7·2%)
2 meals	60 143 (53·5%)	75 445 (42·2%)
3 meals	13 917 (12·4%)	32 431 (18·1%)
4 meals	8199 (7·3%)	15 364 (8·6%)
5 meals	15 741 (14·0%)	33 920 (19·0%)
6 meals	1592 (1·4%)	2734 (1·5%)
7 meals	1361 (1·2%)	6052 (3·4%)

The increase in total meals served has benefited an extra 66 457 people (Table 2). However if there had not been the trend to serve a higher proportion of 3–7 meals at the expense of a lower proportion of 1–2 meals, *more people* could have benefited: at a conservative estimate, an extra 25 000 people.

Although the most common number of meals served in 1978/9 was still 2 per week (and Portsmouth has retained that level of delivery), just over half the people served received three meals or more and 32% of the total received four meals or more. There was a notable increase in the proportion receiving 5 or 7 meals-on-wheels per week. This partly reflects the expressed ideal of some authorities to join the ranks of those who deliver 5 per week, or 'better still, every day'. It may also reflect the fact that there is a shortage of residential care, resulting in more ageing and dependent people remaining in the community; the average age in Local Authority residential homes for the elderly is rising, and is now nearly 82 years. Therefore some meals-on-wheels organisers feel that their resources must be used mainly to meet the needs of very dependent people.

However, because Local Authorities do not have a uniform and simple means of assessment of need, or re-assessment of need, it could be that some of those receiving five or seven meals-on-wheels could not only manage with less, but would benefit from some of the alternative services in the borough and would thereby gain more social contact and increased independence. In our survey many recipients who were without doubt physically, emotionally and environmentally handicapped *did not want*, and by our assessment did not need, more than two meals-on-wheels per week.

Obviously there are many who could not manage without five or seven meals per week. But there are also many who would benefit enormously from just one delivered meal per week. In itself, one meal cannot be of great nutritional value in the context of a week's total diet. But this one delivered meal may give a new incentive and thus introduce and help maintain a healthy pattern of eating. By introducing a greater number of people to one delivered meal a week, the net of Social Services could be spread wider to include those not at present on the list. Remember that 200 meals can reach 40 people five times a week, but 200 people once a week. The needs of these recipients could be kept under review by such weekly contact.

There are many problems in organising a flexible delivery round. We all know there is difficulty in recruiting drivers and deliverers of meals-on-wheels; and that fuel costs are escalating. Can any of these difficulties be overcome? One possibility is to deliver only twice weekly to those in need of 4 meals: on say, Monday and Thursday deliver an extra meal to be eaten on the Tuesday and Friday; or on Friday, deliver for the week-end. The type of meal envisaged could be boil-in-the-bag, bacteriologically safe even if stored unrefrigerated. This is already being considered in some areas. Another possibility is to mount a strong recruitment drive for volunteer meals-on-wheels deliverers among the ranks of the recently retired. It is certain that by resisting a possible cut-back in the service of meals-on-wheels the Local Authority will be saving the far more costly provision of domiciliary care.

Re-assessment of present meals-on-wheels recipients could find many who would be better with luncheon clubs or other types of help. Since 1970 there has been a doubling in number of meals served 'elsewhere' i.e. at luncheon clubs and day centres, from nearly 7½ million in 1970 to nearly 15 million in 1978/9. Again, as is shown in Table 1, the main increase had taken place by 1974, followed by a levelling off. In 1978 there were in England over 4000 centres and clubs serving meals, of which 62% were open for service on 1–2 days, 34% on 3–5 days, and 4% on 6–7 days. Again, for many of the diners the limiting factor is often the problem of transport, particularly as the drivers find some handicapped elderly people may not be ready on time, and cannot be hurried.

The UK services of meals-on-wheels and luncheon clubs are unparalleled in the world. But are we still anywhere near the target of reaching all who are in need of the service, and bringing to each one the greatest individual benefit?

4
Meals-on-wheels in the United Kingdom

Although some authors have in a wider context made passing and often complimentary allusions to meals-on-wheels there are, as shown in Chapter 2, very few detailed reports about these delivered meals.

Indeed, when one is asked by foreign visitors (or even by one's own compatriots) about 'meals-on-wheels in the UK', it is necessary first to claim modestly that the UK leads the rest of the world in its meals-on-wheels service; then to explain that there are no standards for the delivered meal!

One cannot fill the questioner's note book with neat statistics of costs, food values, distances travelled or cooking processes. One admits, somewhat apologetically, that meals-on-wheels are hard to define. This chapter will show that they vary from one district and even from one town to another in:

those eligible for meals-on-wheels	cost
numbers delivered	menus and recipes
frequency of receipt	portion size
source	administration

As part of the explanation of this it is helpful to look at the history of meals-on-wheels, as reported by Dame Susan Walker, former Deputy Chairman of the WRVS*:

> During the second world war, the WVS was involved in attempts to provide easily accessible sources of ration-free food which by 'collective' cooking made the most of our limited supplies. Some 17000 members of the WVS were working in what were called Communal Feeding Centres.

---

*WRVS — Women's Royal Voluntary Service, formerly known as WVS — Women's Voluntary Service.

The Minister of Food (Lord Woolton) agreed to take on these centres as the responsibility of the Ministry of Food, so long as the 17 000 WVS continued to work in them.

Mr Churchill decided that the centres should be renamed 'British Restaurants'. They operated on the basis of giving extra meals with a good meat content (without taking any coupons from the individual's ration book) to the people of the locality. Hundreds of British Restaurants were set up all over the country.

For the agricultural worker, doing hard physical work, the WVS later suggested to the Ministry of Food the setting up of an Agricultural Pie Scheme. They were supplied with the requisite rations and with the full responsibility for the scheme.

It started on a very small scale. Pies were cooked in private houses. According to the area this could be a vicarage kitchen, a member's own small kitchen or the kitchen of a large house. They were delivered by private cars to the people working on the land and sold to them at a price which would not undercut local shops. The profits benefited local schemes, from bus shelters to maternity hospitals.

Before long millions of pies were being delivered by private cars and 'from John O'Groats to Land's End they varied in content.'

The principle of cooking and carrying individual *meals* developed in the urban districts. Dame Susan Walker recalls that:

By 1946 the meals were kept hot by using wooden hay-boxes, old blankets, old felt hats, a consignment of Canadian Red Cross dinner pails and any other devices which would help to retain heat. Ten years later, charcoal heated Hotlocks were in use and despite trials with atomic energy, electricity, gas and a wide variety of devices, the old familiar Hotlock — though with modifications — is still amongst the most efficient heaters, often to the amazement of those who approach the problem from the outside. However, better methods are still being sought.

To begin with, human carriers (on foot) were most often used for transportation. The first 'wheels' were on perambulators and bicycles, and then cars and vans whenever petrol was available. Nowadays special vans or private cars are generally the 'wheels' but in bad weather the meals can, and do, arrive on skis, toboggans and even canoes.

By 1947 approximately 6000 meals a week were being served, as well as large quantities of hot (but non-statistical) soup.

By 1957 numbers of meals served per annum by the WVS had risen to over one million.

In 1962, legislation empowered Local Authorities to provide capital finance for kitchens, transport and containers, and nowadays Local Authorities and paid workers are augmenting, or sometimes taking over, the work of the voluntary organisations.

But the enormous expansion of meals-on-wheels is still making large demands in terms of volunteer involvement. One major problem is how to find enough people to deliver a meal, when the one most eagerly accepted is the midday delivery. In spite of increasing economic and family pressures which occupy the working day of women and men, volunteers are still being found, in the great majority of cases from the ranks of the 45–65 year olds, men as well as women; plus of course the essential and considerable contribution from other organisations such as Red Cross, Women's Institutes, Townswomen's Guilds, British Legion, Council of Churches and many others.

Those Eligible for Meals-on-Wheels

The DHSS (Circular 5/70) recommended that 'those who receive meals-on-wheels should be the elderly or handicapped living in their own homes who cannot provide for themselves a hot meal daily and cannot be provided with one in any preferable way'.

It pointed out that the circumstances in which people need help vary very widely and precise criteria for selection are impossible. But it suggested that people needing help will most often be found in the following groups:

1 Those living alone (or alone during the day) who are sick or mentally confused or so physically infirm that they have difficulty in preparing or cooking a main meal.

2 Those in temporary difficulty (e.g. the convalescent or bereaved).

3 Those who have inadequate cooking facilities or have not the will to make proper use of their facilities, but cannot get meals from other sources (e.g. clubs).

Anyone who is thought to be in need of meals-on-wheels can be brought to the notice of the Local Authority by a neighbour, relative or other visitor. They may be reported as being in need by the health or welfare staff of the Authority, by the hospital, or by the doctor. Medical certification of need is not necessary, but when a health problem is involved the doctor may advise, and be kept informed when meals-on-wheels are given or stopped.

Numbers Delivered

The addition of Local Authority to voluntary services played a vital part in growth rates and comprehensive coverage of the meals-on-wheels service.

From what now seems to be the modest 1 million meals delivered in 1957, numbers had risen by 1972 to nearly 20 million meals-on-wheels delivered in the United Kingdom (England, Wales, Scotland and Northern Ireland).

In Table 2 (p.19) we have confined our figures to England (figures for the whole of the UK are not always easily comparable at specific dates), but these figures are sufficient to show the continued increase in total deliveries, and the trend towards the delivery of an increasing proportion of 3–5 meals per week and a decreasing proportion of 1–2 meals per week.

Frequency of Receipt

Three important nutritional surveys of the elderly, conducted by King Edward's Hospital Fund in 1965, 1971 and 1972, stated that there is no significant contribution to the nutritive value of the dietary when fewer than 4 meals-on-wheels a week are provided. (They point out that the nutritive value of the meals is of course of importance.)

The DHSS Circular 5/70 does not dispute these recommendations. It states:

> It should be clearly understood by all concerned that meals services make a significant contribution to nutrition only if they assure to the consumer at least five hot main meals a week.

But what of the next sentence? I wonder whether, in some Local Authorities, it has been misread? Because the DHSS Circular 5/70 continues

> ...meals-on-wheels may *contribute* to this objective by providing a meal on the day or days in the week *when relatives, neighbours, lunch clubs, etc. cannot do so*, or they may have to meet the full need, and the service must therefore be planned and operated *flexibly* (my italics).

Yet in a number of Local Authorities it seems that this DHSS Circular has been translated into a positive and proud goal (reflected in our quoted statistics) of delivering an increasing proportion of 5 meals-on-wheels a week, ideally raising this to 7 delivered meals a week.

The assessment of numbers of meals-on-wheels needed, and wanted, by the individual is generally an intuitive and personal decision. Although many Authorities now attempt to operate a flexible scheme, giving one or two delivered meals for some, and five or more to others, a carefully planned assessment (see Chapter 11) could make fuller use of other local services available (some of them costing the Authority little or nothing).

It has been pointed out in Chapter 3 (and from the evidence in our survey we shall examine this possibility in full detail) that because of the support of just one or two delivered meals-on-wheels in the week, some desperately needy recipients could then manage other meals (and might prefer to manage) for themselves, or with help, on other days.

At present, with delivery services already over-stretched, some Authorities cannot even operate a waiting list. Only the most urgent cases are catered for and the rest cannot be considered for meals-on-wheels. But by an improvement in assessment technique, 5–7 meals could be reserved only for those with special needs and no alternative resources, and even for them swift reassessment could be made of altered circumstances. It might then be possible to offer others the much sought after one or two meals-on-wheels per week, and to re-assess and reduce any waiting lists. It is recognised that although meals-on-wheels are a vital service nutritionally and socially, they are, in the words of the DHSS Circular, 'a second-best service'. The offer of alternatives could bring more happiness, better appetite and a wider outlook to many old people.

Source of Meals
Meals-on-wheels have to be provided in the most effective way to suit the district. They may, for example, come from:

1 *Kitchens belonging to Local Authority or voluntary organisations* These may be used specially for the delivered meals, but kitchens directly under the control of the service are relatively few. In the Portsmouth kitchen of our survey, fuller use was made of premises and staff by cooking on four days a week for two meals-on-wheels delivery rounds, and for spastic recipients on two further days.

2 *Schools* These meals are generally actual school meals — Junior or Senior portions. This arrangement can sometimes pose a great difficulty in finding alternative supplies during school holidays. Present-day cuts or alterations in the School

Meals Service may vitally affect some meals-on-wheels services.

3 *Old people's residential homes*   While they are cooking lunch
for their residents, they may cook extra to be collected for
nearby meals-on-wheels recipients.

4 *Industrial canteens*   Any large firm can encourage its chef to
prepare some extra meals to be collected for a local meals-on-
wheels service. The meals may be the same as those provided
for the firm's staff, or may be varied for meals-on-wheels needs
in size or menu. There may be supply difficulties if the firm
closes down for holidays.

5 *Hospitals*   Hospital kitchens may be asked to provide some
meals (including special diet meals) for a local meals-on-wheels
service.

6 *Restaurants*   Some restaurant owners are willing to cook
meals to be collected for delivery on a meals-on-wheels round.

Cost
In the words of the DHSS Circular 5/70:

> The general practice is to make a fixed charge for meals well
> below cost. It is important that any charge should not be so
> high as to deter elderly people from accepting all the meals
> they need . . . for many elderly people it is important to pay at
> least in part for any such service.

In 1973 the DHSS commissioned a report, *Meals-on-Wheels,
Short Term Study*, from a firm of Management Consultants. In the
6 kitchens visited by these Management Consultants, the actual
total cost of a meal (before charge to recipient) varied from 14·4p to
44·5p. The subsidy varied greatly.

Throughout the UK, the cost to recipients in different districts
shows wide variation. It is affected not only by factors such as
recipes and labour costs, but also by the extent of the subsidy borne
by the Local Authority. Some industrial canteens subsidise meals
they provide for their local senior citizens in the same way as they
subsidise meals for their own workers. In Portsmouth, the cost to
the recipient in 1970 was 2s 6d (subsidy 3d); in 1980 the cost had
risen to 30p (subsidy 30p), but cost to the recipient may soon have
to rise to 50p. Although most recipients consider this good value —
far below what it would cost them to buy a similar two course meal
— when the price rose due to inflation, some expected an upgrade
of menu to reflect the price increase.

Menus and Recipes

There is little nutritional advice available for menus and recipes, although booklets for the guidance of homes and institutions have been published by the King Edward's Hospital Fund, 1965 and the DHSS, 1975. The WRVS have a small handbook for the guidance of those producing meals-on-wheels and luncheon club meals. In practice, the source of the meals is so varied that it is not surprising that supervisors and cooks produce widely differing recipes, frequently with limited nutritional knowledge.

A number of Authorities have switched to, or are considering incorporating, frozen meals, convenience foods, microwave cooking and other manufacturers' suggestions which they hope may reduce labour, cut costs and improve menus and nutritional value.

Portion Size

One of the recommendations of the Management Consultants' Report was that bulk frozen foods, in portions of 10, help to keep down costs through correct portioning. However they later drew attention to the fact that one kitchen was providing 9 portions and another 14 portions using the same pack in the same menu. The lack of portion control – which affects nutrition as well as cost – is considered in Chapter 8.

Administration

The meals-on-wheels scheme, which began as a voluntary service, now varies in the degree of responsibility between Local Authority and voluntary bodies according to the area. Overall in England, Local Authorities provided just over half the Meals served in 1978/9. An Age Concern research document (1978) records that one entire region, East Anglia, and 22 out of 101 Local Authorities in 1975/6 relied entirely on voluntary effort for the provision of meals-on-wheels. In contrast, in the South East only 46·3% of total provision was voluntary and in six London boroughs the service was run entirely by the Local Authority.

The extent to which Local Authorities have taken the responsibility for the service of meals-on-wheels was shown in the previous chapter: whereas in 1970 Local Authorities in England were serving nearly 5 million meals-on-wheels, by 1978/9 this figure had risen to nearly 14 million.

WHAT IS THE FUTURE?

Those are some of the difficulties — and the diversities — of the present UK meals-on-wheels service. In many Authorities, the question now being asked is: Should our future aim be an extension to a 5 day a week service, or possibly even a 7 day service? With ever-increasing costs, perhaps a more urgent issue is, 'At today's — or tomorrow's — prices, how can we ensure the provision of enjoyable, nourishing meals?'

Without doubt, there will still be very many — and probably increasing numbers with the ageing population — who need 5–7 delivered meals a week; but others on the list may prefer alternatives.

The 5 Meals a Week Service

Twenty years ago Amelia Harris, investigating the 499 meals-on-wheels schemes at that time run almost entirely by voluntary organisations, found that:

1 in every 5 schemes provided meals on one day a week only
2 in every 5 schemes provided meals on two days a week
only 21 people were getting a delivered meal every day
One third of the schemes closed down for some part of the year.

Miss Harris made the point that the number of days a scheme operates, while controlling the maximum number of meals that can be given to any recipient, does not necessarily control the minimum number of meals. A scheme operating for 5 days, serving 200 meals a week, may give:

200 people one meal;
100 people two meals;
only 40 people five meals.

The DHSS Meals-on-Wheels Short Term Study (1973) worked on the assumption that 5 meals-on-wheels per week should be given to each recipient. However, it may even be that some pensioners, not actually on a waiting list, would like to receive meals-on-wheels if given the opportunity. This question was broached in the DHSS Nutrition Survey of the Elderly (1972):

> When the 800 subjects not receiving meals-on-wheels were asked whether they would like to receive them, 35 (4·4%) said they would, the proportion being similar in all the six areas surveyed.

The position was summed up at that time by Professor A.N. Exton-Smith, Professor of Geriatric Medicine at University College Hospital, London:

It must be borne in mind that the real need for meals-on-
wheels is much greater than that represented by the 1·5% of
the elderly population at present receiving them.

By 1978/9 the percentage of the elderly population receiving
meals-on-wheels had risen to 2·5–3·0%. But is the real need still
greater, and still not being met?

In order to increase deliveries to five per week for the present
number of recipients (this did not of course take into account that
greater potential number of recipients), the writers of the Management Consultants' Report in 1973 recommended increasing the
speed of service. They would do this by having the meal delivered,
but seldom 'wasting time' in serving it. This recommendation is
alarming in that it would eliminate the

close contact between the elderly and handicapped people
receiving meals and those supplying meals, which is essential if
the food is to be enjoyed and waste avoided. Those who could
help with communications are the workers who deliver meals
... (Stanton 1971).

To maintain cost effectiveness in a 5 meals a week scheme, the
Management Consultants strongly recommended the use of bulk-
frozen and individually frozen meals (while admitting to many
limitations and high costs — the price to be offset against kitchen
costs). They placed a somewhat naive trust in discount buying and
contract buying, but their report serves to illustrate the difficulties
in time and cost that have to be faced in setting up a 5 meals-on-
wheels a week service.

Other countries turn to the United Kingdom, as pioneers of the
meals-on-wheels service, for advice. Recent enquiries received by
the London headquarters of the WRVS have come from Argentina,
Australia, Bermuda, Canada, Germany, Holland, India, Japan,
New Zealand, Portugal, the Seychelles, Switzerland, Turkey and
the USA.

Advice for the service both at home and abroad has to be practical
and workable, according to facilities and resources available. Some
countries wishing to establish or extend meals-on-wheels may be
daunted by the prospect of the service of 5–7 meals-on-wheels per
week. This may result in mistakenly rejecting the whole scheme
rather than starting with a more practical number of two per week,
or even one.

5
A dietary survey on a group of elderly people

This chapter describes the methodology of our survey, which others may wish to follow or adapt.

THE SURVEY

The Survey District — the importance of full co-operation
It is essential in any survey to choose a good team who can work in harmony with each other, the Local Authority and with the subjects participating.

The leader of our team of investigators, Kate Hastrop, was appointed because of her experience in similar work with the DHSS. As she lived in Portsmouth, an area providing two meals-on-wheels a week, and already had good contacts with the social services in that town, it was decided that Portsmouth Authorities should be approached and permission sought to make them the Survey District.

The choice of Mrs Hastrop as the leader of our investigators could not have been bettered. It was her enthusiasm and ability, backed by her team, which achieved close co-operation with the Medical Officer of Health, the Director of Welfare Services, the Women's Royal Voluntary Service (WRVS) organiser and volunteers, the meals-on-wheels kitchen staff and the subjects themselves.

How Many Subjects and How Long the Survey?
Portsmouth had been one of the areas investigated in 1968 for the DHSS Survey of the Elderly (published in 1972) so their figures for Portsmouth would be available for comparison with ours. But we would not merely be repeating the DHSS work as only two of their Portsmouth subjects happened to be in receipt of meals-on-wheels.

At the time, 325 men and women in Portsmouth over the age of 65 were receiving meals-on-wheels twice weekly, on either Monday and Thursday, or Tuesday and Friday. It was estimated that *over the period of one year* (which would take account of seasonal differences in food intake) *the diet of 100 subjects* (i.e. approximately one in three) *could be investigated*. The following were recorded: (a) a week's weighed and recorded diet, (b) information about the delivered meals, including some analysis and (c) socioeconomic background.

Is a Week's Weighed Diet Acceptable?

It is sometimes debated whether a dietary survey made in a single week can indicate what happens in other weeks. However the DHSS had already investigated this problem. Their survey of the elderly showed that a week's weighed diet gave results which were consistent when the subject took part in a second week's weighed diet survey sometime later. Those who had high intakes during the course of only one week had consistently high intakes in their second investigation. Likewise those who showed a low nutrient intake during the course of only one week showed similar intakes on a reappraisal. They concluded that

> 'as a validation of the method of diet recording this was a reassuring finding'.

Learning From Others

Before finalising the design of our survey, preliminary talks were held with designers of other surveys of the elderly (Government Social Survey; King Edward's Hospital Fund; DHSS), so that the methods and questionnaires of this survey would be in line with theirs and would avoid problems which they had already overcome. For example the diet balance scale read to ⅙ oz as recommended by DHSS; ⅓ oz was found to be insufficiently accurate.

Establish Their Aims Before You Can Criticise their Results!

The Local Authority

In order to investigate the adequacy of the meals-on-wheels service in Portsmouth, its aims were first determined, knowing that the aims differ with different Local Authorities. In some areas the aim is open to wide and rather vague interpretation, for example 'meals-on-wheels should provide a hot, nutritious meal to those who could not otherwise obtain one'. Incidentally, this use of the term 'nutritious' is particularly vague.

According to the Portsmouth Director of Welfare Services the aims of the Portsmouth Meals-on-Wheels service were:

1 To give the nutritional benefit of at least 2 meals per week to those completely housebound.
2 To satisfy a temporary need, e.g. return from hospital or incapacity due to an injury.
3 To give regular social contact, help to identify deterioration and to introduce other welfare services.

This last point emphasised the importance of a comprehensive social questionnaire.

The Kitchen Supervisor
The points which influenced the supervisor's choice of menu for the delivered meal were noted. The primary factor was that the dish should travel well. Items were chosen that clients might not otherwise eat because they are too expensive (e.g. roasts) or too much trouble to cook for one (e.g. steak and kidney pie). The supervisor said she was influenced by remembering what her own parents liked in their later years.

How Long/Short is a Good Questionnaire?
We first visited a few pensioners to gain a general picture of meal patterns, shopping difficulties and food preferences. But it was found that either the elderly subjects tired and gave quick answers which they thought would satisfy the investigator and stop further questioning, or else that they were so garrulous because of loneliness that the investigator was exhausted after three hours of unproductive 'chat' whilst the subject was 'as bright as a button'.

We therefore decided to limit our Survey questionnaires to absolute essentials. This may seem obvious, but when formulating a questionnaire it is always tempting to add more questions. For example, it would have been interesting not only to find the previous occupation of the subject (often noted in the case history), but also that of the subject's father, to see whether a change of social class had affected eating habits. Although interesting, this was not considered essential and so it was regretfully but deliberately omitted.

Questions on income and savings are an invasion of privacy and may deter people from co-operating; the only specific question of this nature was 'Are you on supplementary benefit?' This question was left to the end so that all the other information wanted had already been gathered should the subject decide not to answer further questions. However, because of the rapport established by the end of the week other financial information was often forth-coming.

Preliminary Trials can Save Time and Confusion Later

Special emphasis was placed in this survey on the ascorbic acid content of meals-on-wheels because vitamin C is often used, even if incorrectly, as an index of the quality of the meals. We were also interested in a possible relationship between depression and potassium intake. In the preliminary trials, analyses of vitamin C and potassium were conducted by myself, but once all the supervision and evaluation of the survey started, the analyses were carried out at the laboratory of the City Analyst in Portsmouth.*

We also practised a preliminary 'run through' at the kitchen: to avoid interference with usual kitchen routine a rehearsal of the kitchen duties of the investigators was conducted. The investigators had previously been trained in methodology by the leader of the team. It was considered important that they should not hinder kitchen staff or delay the speed of service. Meals taken by the investigator for analysis were paid for in order to avoid any financial loss to Portsmouth.

The Pilot Survey

When the questionnaires had been formulated, a pilot survey was carried out on 10 subjects, i.e. 5 men and 5 women over 65 years of age receiving two meals-on-wheels per week in Portsmouth. The time period of the pilot survey was December 1969 to February 1970. The main investigation took place between May and November 1970.

Results of the Pilot Survey

From the pilot survey it was apparent that four investigators would be needed for the sample of 100 subjects. In a number of instances the recipient lived several miles from the kitchen. In the pilot survey the investigators had timing and transport difficulties travelling between the kitchen, city analyst, and subject. It was therefore

---

*My first ascorbic acid assays at Queen Elizabeth College, using the Indophenol Method of Oliver and Harris, had shown difficulties with foods such as carrots and prunes as the estimation relies on the observation of the development of a pale pink colour. It was because of this that we decided to use instead the Potentiometric Indophenol Method of Harris, Mapson and Wang (1942), which does not depend on colour.

decided that the four investigators should work in pairs and that in each pair one investigator should do kitchen duties and visit the city analyst for both of them on the meals-on-wheels day (thus freeing her partner for the rest of the survey work). Her task was to weigh the two subject's meals and then to take duplicate foods to the analyst. On the next meals-on-wheels day the other partner undertook the visiting of kitchen and analyst for both.

It was realised that the sample should be drawn no earlier than three weeks before the start of the experiment, to minimise the loss of subjects through death or illness. The investigators' time schedule allowed sufficient period for a last minute subject replacement to be made if necessary.

Our pilot survey showed that a few subjects would need weekend visits and more than one visit a day to help with the dietary record.

It was decided to add a further four questions to the social questionnaire. These concerned cooking facilities, refrigeration, duration of special diets and the time of the last intake of fluid in the day.

The pilot survey highlighted three points from the dietary record:

1 There was no column for itemising food wastage from meals-on-wheels in the DHSS record book (see Appendix B) which was used for the survey. Where wastage occurred it was essential to record the weight of wastage of the individual foods, thus showing the actual amount consumed.

2 It was helpful to have a book of weights of common food portions which was prepared by the investigators to check the recorded information and to simplify checking the weights of standardised commercial foods

    e.g. 2 digestive biscuits   = 1   oz
          1 slice from large sliced loaf = 1½ oz
          4 large prunes (stoned)   = 2   oz

(Our weighing was in ounces, more familiar weights than grammes to these elderly men and women.)

3 An unexpectedly high figure of ascorbic acid from apple pie was traced to the use of an imported canned apple. Ascorbic acid, used as an anti-oxidant, is sometimes added during the canning process in order to keep the natural white colour of the fruit (cut apples brown in the presence of oxygen). But in this product it also gave a higher vitamin C value than would normally be found in a pie made from fresh cooking apples.

Because of the discovery of this seemingly irrational figure, further details for other foods (including cooking methods) were obtained for the information of the analyst.

It was decided that the frequent meetings between the two investigators during the pilot investigation had been invaluable, and that this practice should continue with the team of four investigators.

The four added questions of the social questionnaire were put to the ten subjects. As the pilot survey had proved satisfactory it was decided to include these subjects' results in the final sample.

To continue the goodwill established with Portsmouth authorities, an interim report showing the results of the pilot survey was sent to those responsible for administering the service, and later a short explanatory talk was given to those concerned.

THE SAMPLE

Past surveys of the elderly had found three main difficulties in obtaining the sample:

1 *Lists provided were found to be incomplete or incorrect.* For example, in King Edward's Hospital Fund for London's *Report of an Investigation into the Dietary of Elderly Women Living Alone* (Exton-Smith and Stanton, 1965) 5 people on the list had to be interviewed to find one who fitted the desired category of a woman between 70 and 80 years living alone.

2 *Refusal of subjects to co-operate.* In the above sample, of those suitable, about 1 in 10 refused to co-operate.

3 *Some subjects were considered unsuitable for the survey.* About 1 in 10 in the King Edward's Hospital Fund survey were unacceptable because they were too deaf or too confused.

Hobson and Pemberton (1955) in Sheffield were provided with a complete list of elderly people from Food Office records. They stated with a representative selection of 1 in 30 of all in the area, but for various reasons had to omit 307 subjects leaving 1087. These were all visited but by the time the work started 18 months later the effective sample had dropped to 618. Some of these refused to take part, leaving 466 to participate. But of these only 332 consented to hospital examination, and only 303 completed the dietary survey. Only 187 completed both examination and survey.

In the DHSS (1972) survey of the elderly, of the total sample of 1568 subjects only 879 finally participated in the study.

Even with our survey, when it would be expected that there would be no difficulty in obtaining a complete up-to-date list of subjects because they were all receiving meals-on-wheels regularly each week, in fact no such list existed. Details of clients were kept in various notebooks, names were entered in the order in which the meals had been requested and records went back for five years. Therefore when a complete list was compiled from these books there were names of people who had since died, moved out of the district, or had become hospitalised.

As shown above, the King Edward's Hospital Fund report had found a high refusal to co-operate even among people who were already chosen to be in the desired category. We had to face the possibility that the drop-out rate in our survey would be higher than that of previous surveys because we purposely made no discrimination as to category: even the confused were approached to participate. Our sample of men and women included the deaf, the confused, the alcoholic, those on special diets and the disabled. It included the physically handicapped and mentally weak as well as the mobile and alert.

Steps Taken in Order to Achieve a Broad Sample

1 In order to get this broad sample a decision was made to exclude biochemical or medical tests so that the elderly men and women were caused the least inconvenience, embarrassment or fear; they were not even asked to give blood samples or to undress for examination. Although biochemical and medical tests would have added a fuller dimension to the survey, and would have been necessary had we been investigating malnutrition (Exton-Smith, 1970), the answers sought about total diet and meals-on-wheels in this survey did not depend on them.

2 The investigator was personally introduced to each subject by the familiar meals-on-wheels deliverer, and an appointment card was sent so that the elderly clients would have no fear of answering the door.

3 Where necessary, relatives were encouraged to discuss the subject's participation.

As a result of these precautions, only nine people who were asked to take part in the survey refused to participate. Reasons for refusal were noted, e.g. embarrassing incontinence. Reasons were varied enough not to have excluded any one particular category of the elderly.

Our Stratified Random Sample

A stratified random sample of 100 people was taken from the 325 persons over the age of 65 years who received meals-on-wheels in Portsmouth. In other words, by this acknowledged method of selection, the 100 subjects would have the same proportion of males to females, with the same age groupings, as in the original 325. The sample consisted of 74 women and 26 men; 24 women and 10 men were between 65 and 74 years and 50 women and 16 men were 75 years and over. It should be noted that the ten subjects in the pilot study were included in this sample.

Although this was a stratified random sample of the recipients of meals-on-wheels in Portsmouth, no claim is made that it represents meals-on-wheels recipients in the country as a whole.

THE INVESTIGATORS AND THE SURVEY TECHNIQUES

The choice of investigators was of prime importance, particularly for this generation of elderly. Our four investigators were Caucasian women, mature and attractive, warm in personality and used to dealing with the elderly and gaining their confidence and friendship.

The investigators met frequently to make sure their survey techniques were standardised. At one early meeting they discussed every question on the questionnaire to make sure that each would be interpreted in the same way by each investigator.

Organisation of the Investigators

Meals-on-wheels were cooked and dished up in the kitchen by the kitchen supervisor and staff on four days, but each subject received only two per week, either on Mondays and Thursdays or on Tuesdays and Fridays.

As mentioned earlier, after the initial pilot study the investigators worked in pairs. Each investigator was responsible for 'kitchen duties' on one day per week in order to save the time and travelling found so inconvenient in the pilot study. 'Kitchen duties' included weighing each item of the meal (meat, gravy, potatoes, vegetables, sweet, pastry in either course and custard or other sauce). The weighing was for the meals of two recipients, the investigator's own subject's meal and that of her fellow investigator. The meals were taken at random during the course of 'conveyor belt' type dishing up by the kitchen staff. The whole meal was then labelled with the recipient's name and address and placed in the appropriate charcoal heated Hotlock, checking that the deliverer was aware of the labelled meals.

After weighing the meals for the two recipients, duplicate samples of foods from the main course and the dessert were collected into foil containers labelled with the name and number of the two subjects eating the comparable meal and the time at which they usually ate the meal. For each subject two samples of main course and two samples of dessert were sent to the analyst in order to give him sufficient material. The type of food and method of preparation and cooking were noted for the analyst's information. (After a few months, when it had been established that some foods, e.g. puddings, gave consistently low readings for ascorbic acid, the average value was recorded for that food, without further analyses. So after the first few months, only vegetables and fruits were sent for ascorbic acid analysis).

The investigator then proceeded immediately to the city analyst's department to deliver the sample food for analysis. The samples to be analysed for ascorbic acid were preserved with metaphosphoric acid to stop any further destruction of the vitamin. A few foods were analysed for potassium in order to check our analysed values against the food tables figures (we were particularly interested in the potassium intake of our subjects because potassium intake has sometimes been correlated with depression). The foods to be analysed for potassium were refrigerated at 4°C, until needed by the analyst.

An Example Time Plan for one Investigator

(Monday as kitchen duty day; pattern is the same for other investigators visiting kitchen on other meals-on-wheels delivery days, i.e. Tuesday, Thursday or Friday.)

Monday
1 Kitchen duties — as described.
2 Visit to analyst — as described.
3 First visit to new subject — often lengthy and unrewarding, while gaining subject's confidence and co-operation.
4 Final visit to previous week's subject to cover complete 7 day week. Additional visits were occasionally necessary when compiling records.

Tuesday
1 Routine visit.
2 Continue to write up work.

Wednesday 1 Routine visit.
              2 Continue to write up work.
Thursday 1 Visit kitchen to accompany WRVS helpers for introduction to possible subjects for ensuing weeks. *Note*: This can often take the whole morning driving from one part of the city to another and discussing the purpose of the survey to gain cooperation from subjects.
              2 Routine visit.
              3 Conclude write-up of previous week.
Friday 1 Routine visit.
              2 Visit new subject to estabish that he or she can commence participation in survey the following Monday. This is important as although agreement may have been made some 2–3 weeks previously, circumstances may well have changed due to illness, holidays, etc. It enables the investigator to arrange visits to another subject without wasting time at the beginning of a week's work.
              3 Start collating information on the next subject for checking on following visit next Monday.
Saturday and Sunday Visit subject, unless this is not needed, i.e. he or she is alert and reliable (or co-operation is given by relative or friend).

Note: It should be made quite clear at this point that no week could really be described as 'typical' and, of even more significance, the investigators had no way of knowing at the commencement of the week's work their possible (voluntary) involvement, e.g. —
    collecting pensions for subject
    collecting prescriptions and medicines
    changing library books
    shopping
    checking accounts for subject (rates, fuel, etc.).

Also: 1 It was often found necessary to check facts given by the subjects against files kept in the Local Authority Welfare Department.
          2 Where medication details were unclear a visit to the subject's GP was needed.

3 Where meals were provided by a relative or friend, often at weekends, a visit to the relative or friend was necessary to enlist their help in order to obtain accurate weights of food.

4 Several subjects regularly visited day centres for lunch and were accompanied by the investigator. It was also found to be well worth visiting the day centre prior to this to gain co-operation from helpers and to explain the purpose of the survey.

THE QUESTIONNAIRES

We had found, during our preliminary investigations, that unnecessary questions had to be eliminated: in surveys of this nature there are already very many essential questions to be answered.

We were fortunate in having the advice of Dr G.W. Lynch (since deceased, formerly lecturer in social nutrition at Queen Elizabeth College) in formulating our questionnaires. We decided to place related topics close together so that the questions could be asked in the form of a guided conversation, not in a question and answer session which many elderly people find extremely trying or intimidating. The pilot study had shown that once the subjects were tired, they tended to give an answer which they thought the interviewer would like to receive. They may also give unrevealing answers if they feel unsympathetic to the interviewer; for example they may not wish to tell the truth to a very young investigator; or to one who conducts a questionnaire in a manner which limits the answer without any allowance for open ended conversation.

Our investigators were instructed not to use a notebook, or a tape recorder, either of which may inhibit relaxed conversation. Instead they were instructed to fill in the obtained answers immediately after the visit but out of the house. They were told that if they doubted the veracity of an answer they should wait until nearer the end of the week when better communication was established.

The decision on the type and content of a questionnaire is of primary importance, particularly when dealing with the very elderly or the confused. An American description of how *not* to question the 'old old' is given in the following anecdote (Schmidt, 1975):

> It had been decided to use a 'morale scale' to assess reactions to statements, and in this way to record the mental status of those in their 80s and 90s. The morale scale used consisted mainly of

short direct statements such as 'things get worse as I get older'. This interviewer found herself shouting at a 90 year old nursing home resident, 'sometimes I worry so much that I can't sleep'. The old woman patted her hand and murmured sympathetically 'I'm so sorry dear' ... After this experience, the statements were re-phrased as questions!

The questionnaires used in our survey are shown in detail in Appendix B. For ease of identification, three colour-sections were used for the questionnaires. Pink paper contained the questions related to the delivered meals; white paper contained socio-economic questions; blue paper contained questions which were not to be coded for the computer.

The first uncoded question involved a 24 hour recall of the type of foods eaten from breakfast through to bedtime. The subject was asked whether the pattern changed on other days or at weekends. The next question asked the approximate amounts of different foods bought each week. A standard list of basic foods was used. The information gained by the 24 hour recall plus the list of weekly purchases was sufficient to check that the answers given in the diet record were likely to be reliable and that special purchases had not been made to impress. At the beginning there was also occasionally a tendency to overestimate or underestimate problems either for sympathy or for reasons of pride.

The uncoded questionnaire was completed at the end of the week by a detailed, confidential case study, which threw light on seemingly irrational answers.

As the coded questionnaires were designed for possible future use by other Local Authorities, some questions to which the answer was already known were coded and included, e.g. Question 4 — How much does the meal cost you? Question 6 — How often do you get them?

Each subject was interviewed daily for at least five days of the investigation week. They were visited 1–2 times a day according to their ability. If the subjects were visiting or being visited at weekends, the host or guest would sometimes replace the investigator for weighing the diet.

THE DIET RECORD

Subjects were taught to record all food and drink consumed for the seven consecutive days. They were issued with a notepad with a page for each day. Each page was divided into headings: Before or on rising; breakfast; mid-morning; mid-day; mid-afternoon; evening; before retiring or in bed.

To weigh the foods, a dietary balance was left with the subjects at the beginning of the investigation week. If they were unable to weigh, relatives were sometimes asked to help, or the investigator either weighed the actual food or a comparable portion on her daily visit or visits. When necessary, weight checks were obtained from friends, relations or shopkeepers or the book of common weights mentioned in the pilot study was used. Larder checks were made unless there was a specific request against.

Meals-on-wheels, twice weekly, were weighed item by item before delivery. After the meal had been eaten, any wastage was itemised and weighed in the home by the investigator. Wastage was recorded in the diet record book. It was made plain to the subject that wastage was of interest for the survey and would not be used as a reason for stopping meals-on-wheels delivery.

The list of food items and their weights was transferred from the subject's notes by the interviewer into the diet record book which was the same as that used by the DHSS (see Appendix B). In this way any obvious omissions could be queried immediately. Each food item was recorded with the appropriate code number by the investigator and rechecked by the leading investigator before final checking at Queen Elizabeth College.

The investigators were asked to comment in the diet record to explain seeming eccentricities. They were also required to give a final assessment of the individual diet records as being (a) reasonably reliable, (b) doubtful, (c) of little validity. All but eight were classed as reasonably reliable.

Very close supervision had to be given to these eight subjects. Two examples are given below:

Subject 24 The subject's son agreed to weigh everything, but the investigator was not convinced of his accuracy and dared not query too many items because the son was known to get very angry (a violent man with a history of mental disorder). On one occasion he hit his mother because she did not eat all the potatoes he had weighed for the survey. The investigator weighed some items and made as many cross-checks as possible.

Subject 48 Although interested, as was her daughter, in the survey, and full co-operation was promised after the scales were demonstrated, this subject failed to keep proper records and was vague. She was unwell during the suvey period and said she normally ate better than during this week. Basic items were weighed by the investigator.

Other problems that needed special vigilance were as follows:

Subject 50   Emotionally disturbed.

Subject 51   Very disinterested in food.

Subject 71   Eating food from husband's plate in addition to her own.

Subject 88   Food dropped on floor due to failing eyesight.

Subject 95   Unable to weigh, and unco-operative when investigator wanted to do it for her.

Subject 96   Gave food away and received food and was unco-operative about giving information.

It is of interest that it was felt that reliable results were obtained from the other subjects, including those normally considered to be difficult for inclusion in a weighed diet programme with questionnaires, e.g. the deaf, alcoholic, blind, slightly confused, those on special diet. But it was essential to have a good team of patient, trained investigators.

6

Measuring nutrient intake

Statistics are like bikinis. What they reveal is interesting, but what they conceal is fascinating.

USING THE COMPUTER

For those who are not familiar with food surveys, this chapter considers some of the figure-work normally used for weighed and recorded diet surveys.

In a week's weighed diet it is important to discourage the subjects, or those doing the weighings for them, from becoming slapdash. Therefore, all items of food and drink consumed must be weighed with meticulous accuracy — in our survey to one-sixth of an ounce (i.e. 0·17 oz, or less than 5 grams). To calculate the diet, these weighed foods, i.e. the 'foods eaten', are then translated into 'intakes of nutrients'. To do this, use is made of Food Tables which give the nutrient composition of foods.

The figures in the Food Tables are the results of years of painstaking analysis of hundreds of different foods either raw, cooked, or combined in recipes. Different samples of the same foodstuff may vary in composition, so the figures in the tables are generally the average obtained from a number of different samples. Where necessary the figures allow for nutrient losses due to cooking.

The Queen Elizabeth College computer (Elliot 903) was programmed by Dr R.H.J. Watson to calculate the nutrient content of foods, based on the Food Tables prepared in the Department of Health and Social Security (1969). These had been used in the DHSS Survey of the Elderly (1972); by using them we would be able to make direct comparisons with that survey. They differed from the Food Tables then most commonly used in the UK, those compiled by McCance & Widdowson (1960), only in that they contained some additional foods and recipes and some slightly different analyses, e.g. animal protein and non-animal protein; also, they were specially prepared for use in surveys of people living in their own homes.

Those who are used to working with computers will know that the translation of 'foods eaten' into 'nutrients consumed' is routine once the master tape has been punched. Even so, for me it is always a memorable moment when entering the computer's lair to find it — as I imagine it — audibly 'eating' the computer tape. Each rapid tick of the machine signifies the 'digestion' of a figure for a number coded foodstuff, with an immediate translation of this foodstuff into its component nutrient columns. In our Survey, these were:

Energy	Added sugar	Pyridoxine (B_6)
Animal protein	Water	Folate
Non-animal protein	Vitamin A	Cobalamin (B_{12})
Total protein	Vitamin C	Sodium
Fat	Vitamin D	Potassium
Carbohydrate	Thiamin (B_1)	Calcium
Protein energy %	Riboflavin (B_2)	Magnesium
Fat energy %	Niacin	Iron
Carbohydrate energy %		

One of the important questions our survey intended to ask was: what part do meals-on-wheels play *in the total diet* of each recipient? So, by a special programming device, the computer was able to recognise separately the foods contributed by each of the delivered meals-on-wheels.

In the computer room I was fascinated to hear that the audible reaction to this program device — the recognition of the input of weighed food items from meals-on-wheels — was not a quick 'tick', but a more dignified slow 'tock'. The computer rapped out quick ticks as it went through one subject's punched tape diet record. This man was a diabetic, a retired medical doctor, then in his 80s who ate little and often. He kept his diet wide; plenty of protein foods, nourishing drinks and a variety of vegetables all prepared lovingly by his elderly French wife.

After what seemed an age of rapid rhythmical 'ticks', I was beginning to experience a waning appetite when, following a brief pause, the computer changed to its slow 'tocks' and I realised we had only just reached lunch time. The computer was 'digesting' the components of the delivered meal. I left the computer room, feeling replete, round about the subject's tea time. For some other subjects, who eat few foods, the computer is able to translate the day's recorded diet into nutrients in just a few minutes.

One important point became obvious as I listened to these 'ticks and tocks': even snack meals were taking their time to be recorded and translated by the computer. Snacks are often referred to as 'only snacks', i.e. not 'proper meals'. But some of these 'only snacks' were contributing valuable nutrients to the daily diets of our elderly men and women.

Table 3
Part of Computer Print-out for One Subject

Day of the Week	Vit A	Vit D
	µg	µg
*Monday	880	1·64
Tuesday	546	1·17
Wednesday	382	0·99
*Thursday	1233	1·87
Friday	341	1·01
Saturday	131	0·05
Sunday	273	1·00

*Includes m/w

Nutrients contributed by Meals-on-Wheels (m/w)

Monday's m/w	584	0·63
Thursday's m/w	903	0·47

(Also shown on print-out but not included in this table: intakes for groups of days, i.e. m/w days, other weekdays, all weekdays, weekends and whole week.)

Table 3 shows a sample of the type of print-out we obtained for each subject. It shows only two of the vitamins. Immediately you can see that, for this subject, an important contribution of vitamins A and D was made by meals-on-wheels. There were equally detailed print-outs for every nutrient on the computer's programme. We could thus see all the nutrients provided (or lacking) in the delivered meals and in every day or groups of days, such as weekends.

However, even before the punching of the computer tapes, the diet recorded needed to be checked by the investigator and by myself. This routine verification often gave fascinating glimpses into the lifestyles of these highly individual people.

For instance, in one diet record book of a 77 year old woman, the investigator had written 'incredible mixture but correct'. She was referring to:

> Tuesday, 10.30 p.m. a cup of tea
> sweetened Horlicks (made with milk)
> bread and milk (also sweetened)
> a fresh orange, sprinkled with sugar
> olive oil

(The weight of each item was recorded in the diet book).

This repast was enjoyed each evening, usually between 10.30 p.m. and midnight, although on the other nights of the survey week the cup of tea was omitted. The two teaspoons of olive oil were taken as a medicine. Other medicines taken by this same woman included Senokot (an aperient), black pellets for indigestion, a 'stomach mixture', a pain killer and quinine (possibly for night cramps).

I found a puzzle in another diet record: could this really be accurate? '2 a.m. : glacé mint, cream cracker, glass of rum.' Answer given in the record 'He was listening to the results of the election and was celebrating the victory of his chosen candidate'.

We had one striking example of the computer, not the investigator, picking up an answer that we could not at first understand. It concerned a figure for the average daily intake of vitamin D for subject 12. How could it be that she had the highest recorded vitamin D intake of all our men and women, and yet had not been eating any foods rich in vitamin D? Our double check of her week's dietary record had shown that she did not eat any margarine, eggs, fatty fish, liver — could it be that the computer was in error? If so, were the figures of the entire survey suspect or even invalid?

I called for the dietary record for a final unhappy check. Indeed this subject was not consuming the main vitamin D foods, but she was sweetening her daily cups of tea with Glucodin. In the Food Tables this had a separate code number from sugar and glucose. The reason was that Glucodin is a product fortified with vitamin D. The computer had automatically picked up from the Food Tables what we might have missed. It had correctly nominated subject 12 as 'highest vitamin D'.

ANALYSES

Vitamin C

It would be foolish to accept blindly Food Tables figures under certain circumstances. For instance, Food Tables figures for ascorbic acid (vitamin C) are notoriously inaccurate under conditions of large scale catering and where there are long periods between cooking and consumption (Platt *et al.*, 1963). We therefore considered it necessary to analyse the delivered meals for this vitamin at the approximate time of consumption. The label on the foods taken for ascorbic acid analysis included a note of the subject's usual lunchtime. Until this time the analyst kept the foods at room temperature, thus allowing continuing destruction of the vitamin. At the recorded lunchtime, the foods were treated with metaphosphoric acid to stop any further ascorbic acid destruction prior to analysis. The results of these analyses are discussed in Chapter 8.

Potassium

We were particularly interested in the potassium intakes of our subjects because low potassium intake has sometimes been correlated with depression. Therefore, a few of the foods most commonly served in the Portsmouth meals-on-wheels were analysed for potassium in order to check the Food Tables figures based on those of McCance and Widdowson (1960). It was not considered necessary to analyse many samples (details are given in Chapter 8). The foods chosen to be analysed for potassium were refrigerated at 4°C until needed by the analyst.

Notes on Analytical Methods — All analyses were carried out in duplicate.

Vitamin C The Potentiometric Indophenol Method of Harris, Mapson and Wang (1942) was used. This method analyses reduced vitamin C, but trial analyses for both reduced and total vitamin C satisfied the analyst that, for the types of food used and having been kept warm for such long periods, analysis for reduced vitamin C would give a sufficiently accurate result.

Potassium was analysed using the flame photometer method with the Pye Unicam SP90A Atomic Absorption Spectrophotometer in the flame emission mode, operated according to manufacturer's instructions.

7
The general dietary intake

This chapter starts to look at the figures which emerged from our survey into the dietary of 100 elderly people in Portsmouth.

We wondered whether we would find, in tabulating the figures, that the computer data would endorse the thoughts and arguments about 'the elderly' put forward in the opening chapters of this book; or would our suggestions be refuted by the figures?

Certainly, a glance at Table i (Appendix A page 183) immediately endorses the statement that 'the elderly are not a section of the population but a cross-section'. This table shows, for every nutrient, an enormous variation in the intakes of our 100 subjects. The very wide ranges record that these elderly people differed widely in their eating habits; moreover, some of them had survived to a ripe old age on intakes which appear to be extremely low, compared with group recommendations.

This wide range of intakes is not only shown in our sample of elderly men and women (all living in one district, all considered to be at nutritional or social risk); it was apparent also in the diet records of 879 elderly men and women with more varied backgrounds — some married or with families, some solitary — from 6 different areas of Great Britain (DHSS 1972); wide ranges of nutrient intakes have also been recorded, and remarked upon, in the dietary study of 60 women, all over the age of 70 and living alone (Exton-Smith and Stanton, 1965). And there is no doubt that you would also find wide ranges in nutrient intakes if you studied the diet of, say, housewives aged 45–50; or restricted your survey to schoolboys at primary school; because whatever our age, we are all leading individual lives with different eating patterns which result in wide ranges of nutrient intake.

Selected dietary intake figures of our Survey are shown in Tables i–iii (Appendix A, p.183–5). There was no marked overall difference in the average nutrient intakes between the different age groups, as shown in Tables ii and iii. There were few exceptions to this: we found a significant fall with advancing age, *for women only*, in intakes of iron, and the percentage of protein. Also the higher average vitamin C intake in our small sample of over 85s was influenced by one subject regularly taking a blackcurrant drink rich in vitamin C.

Next, what of the argument referred to in Chapter 4 that fewer than 4 meals-on-wheels per week are of little nutritional significance? Were we right in suggesting that the provision of only two meals-on-wheels can enable some elderly people to manage on other days? In seeking an answer, it was to our advantage that the DHSS Nutrition Survey of the Elderly was conducted at about the same time as our own (QEC) Survey. We were therefore able to compare our nutrient intake figures with theirs: we found that they were in close agreement. For full details of the comparison, turn to Table iv (Appendix A, page 186).

The 879 DHSS subjects included only 21 to whom meals-on-wheels were delivered. It was interesting to observe from Table iv that our subjects, all of whom were considered to be at sufficient nutritional risk to receive meals-on-wheels, were on average achieving (with only 2 delivered meals per week) about the same average nutrient intakes as the elderly population in the survey by the DHSS.

It should, however, be noted that, as a group, intakes of the younger men (65 to 74 years) in our sample were generally below the DHSS levels.

Table 4 (page 52) gives the 1979 recommended daily amounts for elderly groups in the UK. Some of these figures have been slightly altered from the recommendations current at the time of our survey (DHSS, 1969); the 1969 figures are shown in parenthesis.

In our survey in 1970 (see Table iv, Appendix A) the average energy intakes for women, as well as for the 65–74 year old men, seemed to be below the recommended amounts. Some of these younger men had been dependent on their wives for the provision of meals and had not yet adapted to their solitary state. It is noteworthy that a higher proportion of men than women said they would welcome more than two delivered meals each week. We also recorded case studies of a number of women who found it difficult to manage for themselves on days when meals-on-wheels were not delivered. It is the individual, not the group, that has to be assessed

Table 4

Recommended Daily Amounts of Food Energy and some Nutrients
for Population Groups in the UK
(from DHSS Report, 1979; figures in parenthesis represent
1969 recommendations)

The Older Age Groups—Assuming a Sedentary Life

	Men		Women	
	65–74	75 & Over	55–74	75 & Over
Energy (kcal)	2400	2150	1900	1680
	(2350)	(2100)	(2050)	(1900)
(MJ)	10·0	9·0	8·0	7·0
	(9·8)	(8·8)	(8·6)	(8·0)
Protein (g)	60	54	47	42
	(59)	(53)	(51)	(48)
Thiamin (mg)	1·0	0·9	0·8	0·7
(vitamin B_1)	(0·9)	(0·8)		
Riboflavin (mg)	1·6	1·6	1·3	1·3
(vitamin B_2)	(1·7)	(1·7)		
Nicotinic acid (mg)	18	18	15	15
Total Folate (µg)	300	300	300	300
Ascorbic acid (mg) (vitamin C)	30	30	30	30
Vitamin A (µg retinol equiv.)	750	750	750	750
Vitamin D (µg cholecalciferol)	* (2·5)	* (2·5)	* (2·5)	* (2·5)
Calcium (mg)	500	500	500	500
Iron (mg)	10	10	10	10

*A footnote to the 1979 table includes the recommendation that adults with
inadequate exposure to sunlight, for example those who are housebound,
may need a supplement of 10µg (400 i.u.) vitamin D daily.

for the possible need for extra meals-on-wheels. In the Energy
section of the next chapter the computer data is looked at to see
whether the provision of extra meals-on-wheels would necessarily
raise the energy intakes of all recipients.

Another discrepancy worth noting in Table iv is that in the DHSS
survey the vitamin D intakes of the women only were relatively
low; while in our QEC survey, vitamin D figures for both sexes
were low, even lower than in the DHSS survey. These figures are

discussed more fully in the next chapter (see section on vitamin D).

The conclusion drawn from this investigation into the dietary intake of this group of elderly people would be that for most nutrients the total diet met the recommendations, when one considers *average* intakes and, of course, average intakes can give an important measure of group health. However, attention must be drawn to the figures at the low end of the *ranges*. Table i (page 183), readily shows that quoting only average intakes can give an artificial impression of satisfactory nutritional status. This is often not fully appreciated: it is not possible to study the nutritional data and state categorically whether for an individual (as distinct from a group of subjects) intakes are a sign of an adequate or inadequate diet.

It must be recognised that the nutrient intake figures are based on food tables calculations; these only give an average nutrient content for each food or recipe. The Recommendations (DHSS 1969, 1979) with which one compares these figures, are recommendations for groups of the population. Requirements for you, or for any other individual, are not known; they would need to take into account not only age, sex and activity, but also individual body metabolism, absorption, adaptation, physical state, drug therapy and other factors.

From the nutritional data, it can only be concluded that the average diet of our subjects was adequate and that particularly low intakes of some nutrients merit further investigation.

8
Nutrients of special interest (with particular reference to delivered meals)

Having studied the diet in general it was evident that a few nutrients were of particular concern. We saw apparently low average intakes of vitamin D and potassium and, especially in women, energy and iron. Because of variations in portion size, the delivered meals provided wide ranges of protein and energy. Cooking practices and delivery delays markedly affected intakes of vitamin C.

Blood samples were deliberately omitted from our survey to minimise the number of people who might refuse to take part. Due to this it was not feasible to make assumptions about the effect of the low intakes of iron found in many individuals in this survey. But, as the following pages show, we proceeded to look in fuller detail at vitamin C, vitamin D, potassium, energy and protein.

The illustrations in the text include examples of nutritionally accurate cartoons, produced by the Gerontology Nutrition Unit, Queen Elizabeth College, London, to explain nutrition to elderly audiences, and those concerned with the care of the elderly.

VITAMIN C

In our survey we found some elderly subjects avoided vitamin C foods and had low intakes of vitamin C. Many of the reasons given below also apply to younger age groups:

- Some of the main vitamin C foods are expensive.
- Many found oranges too troublesome to peel.
- Others complained that fruits sting sore gums or lips; some, not realising that the acids in fruits become alkaline in the body, felt that fruits are acid and therefore 'bad for my rheumatism'.

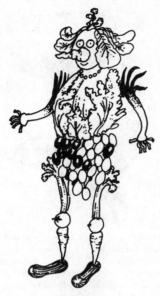

One of the main functions of vitamin C (ascorbic acid) is to assist in the formation of connective tissue, the 'cement' between the cells, in all parts of the body.

Gross deficiency of vitamin C results in scurvy. The patient feels feeble and listless. There is a disturbance in the structure of connective tissue, leading to haemorrhages into the skin and elsewhere; spontaneous bruising; failure of wounds to heal; breakdown of old scar tissues; infection and swelling of the gums.

Scurvy is best remembered as the fatal disease of old time sailors who were at sea for many months on their voyages, away from fresh fruit and vegetables. Dr James Lind, a British Naval surgeon, proved that there was a simple remedy for the disease: citrus fruit. At the end of the eighteenth century, all British sailors were issued with a regular ration of citrus juice — British sailors were nicknamed 'Limeys' — and scurvy was abolished from the British Navy.

Nowadays, scurvy is seen in its severe form mostly in patients ill enough to be hospitalised. There have, however, been suggestions that deficiency of ascorbic acid is not uncommon among elderly people (Taylor, 1968). Diagnostic criteria vary, and only a few cases of scurvy were reported in the DHSS Surveys of the Elderly (1972, 1979). The condition is sometimes referred to as 'Widower's Scurvy', thus named because widowers (and other old people) may lose interest in food and find the preparation of fruits, potatoes and other vegetables too much bother, thereby excluding the main vitamin C foods. Moreover, there is some evidence that elderly subjects have a reduced capacity for absorption of ascorbic acid from the gastrointestinal tract, and this would exacerbate the problem.

- Pips, e.g. of blackcurrants, may work their way painfully under dentures. Unfortunately, some of the easier to eat, popular fruits, e.g. canned peaches, are a poor source of vitamin C.
- Many of our subjects drank orange or lemon squashes unaware that the brand they used contained none of the vitamin C one might expect from an orange or lemon drink.
- There were some complaints that raw salad vegetables are indigestible.
- Greens were often said to cause flatulence.
- Shopping difficulties sometimes led to over-long storage and wilting of fruits and vegetables.
- Poor cooking methods led to unnecessary loss of vitamin C.
- The two delivered meals-on-wheels were sometimes relied on as a main source of fruits and vegetables.

How much Vitamin C is Needed?

When vitamin C intake is low, the individual should be encouraged to take fresh supplies at least 2 or 3 times a week, preferably every day.

To quote from the DHSS Recommended Intakes (1969)

> There have long been two views on the need for ascorbic acid. One view maintains that an amount of the vitamin sufficient to prevent signs of deficiency, and with a safety margin to allow for individual variation and for stresses of everyday life, can be recommended as a dietary intake. The other view is based on the concept of tissue saturation. The argument is that animal species which are able to synthesize their own ascorbic acid (i.e. all except primates, the guinea pig and the fruit bat) maintain tissue saturation. For man, this requires an intake of at least 60 mg/day. There is so far no evidence that man derives any benefit from such a high intake of ascorbic acid.
>
> USA authorities have for long advocated the desirability of tissues being kept close to saturation, and have recommended accordingly (NRC, 1964).

(More recently, 1974, the National Research Council, USA amended their recommendation from 75 to 45 mg/day. It has now been further revised, and elevated to 60 mg/day.)

In the new recommended daily amounts (DHSS, 1979), the UK recommendations for ascorbic acid (30 mg) are still based on an amount sufficient to prevent signs of deficiency, with an added safety margin. The report states that the available data provide no reason to alter this recommendation or to make any change in it for the sex of the subject or for differences in physical activity or increasing age.

Effect of Age on Ascorbic Acid Intake

We found, as did Exton-Smith and Stanton (1965), that the mean daily calculated intake of ascorbic acid fell with advancing age (see Table v, Appendix A, page 187).

If more vitamin C is taken than the body needs, the excess is excreted in the urine. This was thought to be a harmless method of regulation by nature. However, recently the taking of large doses of ascorbic acid has been advocated for optimum health and, it is suggested, for the prevention of colds. The amounts recommended have been measured in grams — far stronger than generally found in foods. There are reports on possible side effects of such large amounts, so at this stage one should be highly cautious about advocating 'megadoses', either as an alternative or in addition to vitamin C foods.

It is all too easy to have vitamin C and other nutrients 'robbed' from fruits and vegetables. The main losses occur when:

1 *Fruits and vegetables wilt with age.*
2 *They are prepared, cut up or left soaking too long in advance.*
3 *They are over-cooked or re-heated — this is especially destructive if bicarbonate of soda has been added.*
4 *Vegetable cooking is begun in cold water (boiling water destroys the enzyme which would otherwise destroy vitamin C).*
5 *Too much cooking water is used.*
6 *There is a long time lag between cooking and consumption.*

The first five are avoidable, with advice and care, either in small-scale or large-scale cooking, i.e. the advice for boiling vegetables should be: choose fresh vegetables, prepare them at the last possible minute, cook, without bicarbonate of soda, for the shortest possible time in a small amount of boiling water (lid on pan to prevent evaporation). But when meals-on-wheels are being delivered it is obvious that the time lag between cooking and consumption is the most difficult problem to overcome.

Time of Consumption

In Portsmouth the meals were put into individual dishes in the kitchen between 9.15 and 10 a.m., ready for collection by the meals-on-wheels vans. The figures below show the interval between dishing-up and consumption of the 200 meals:

within 2 hours	.....	19 meals
between 2–3 hours	.....	127 meals
between 3–4 hours	.....	40 meals
between 4–5 hours	.....	6 meals
more than 5 hours	.....	3 meals
one day (complete meal)	.....	4 meals
two days (complete meal)	.....	1 meal

Included in these meals were seven partly eaten on the same day and partly eaten on the next day; generally it was the pudding, or part of it, which was kept.

Because of the long delays between dishing-up time and eating, we asked the city analyst to assay the vitamin C in the meals-on-wheels not at the time of collection, or even delivery, but at the time of consumption. As mentioned in Chapter 6, the investigators found the customary lunchtime of each recipient and wrote this on the label of the duplicate samples given to the analyst. Other information given to the analyst included the cooking methods, so any unexpected results would be queried.

The delivered meal was reheated by 77% of the subjects before they ate it but they did so in such an inconsistent manner that it was not practicable to make allowance for this: the duplicate samples

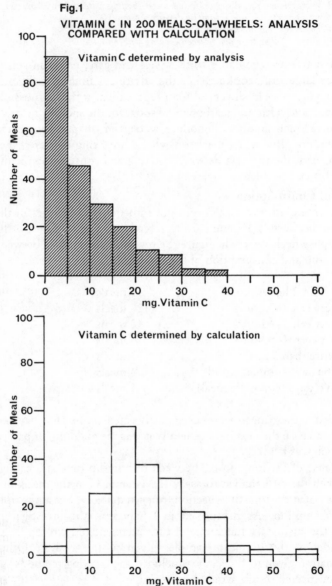

Fig.1

VITAMIN C IN 200 MEALS-ON-WHEELS: ANALYSIS COMPARED WITH CALCULATION given to the analyst were merely kept in the laboratory at room temperature until the normal time of consumption. (The extra destruction of ascorbic acid through the re-heating would have been at this stage very small compared with the time-lag destruction.) The technique of analysis is given in Chapter 6.

Figure I shows the vitamin C value of the 200 meals (two meals-on-wheels per week for 100 subjects) by analysis and by calculation. It can be seen, for example, that by calculation from the food tables only about 15 of the delivered meals contributed less than 10 mg vitamin C; but when analysed, it was found that the true number of delivered meals contributing less than 10 mg was 135.

In domestic cooking there are small losses of vitamin C, even in normal preparation and cooking. These losses are allowed for in the calculated figures, i.e. those taken from food tables.

Platt, Eddy and Pellet (1963) have shown excessive ascorbic acid losses in the large scale cooking practices in hospitals.

Our analysis figures were from meals cooked by large scale practices and then — because of the delays on meals-on-wheels deliveries — kept for long periods before consumption.

It was therefore not surprising that in all but eleven of the 200 meals, the values of ascorbic acid were lower by our own analysis than they were by calculating from the Food Tables. (The high analysis figures in the eleven meals were generally attributable to fortified canned apple.)

Table vi (Appendix A, page 187), shows in detail a comparison of analysed and calculated ascorbic acid contents of some of the vegetables frequently served in the meals-on-wheels. For instance, by analysis at the time of consumption 38 samples of mashed potato showed a mean ascorbic acid content of 1 mg/100 g; the calculated (Food Tables) figure is 10 mg/100 g. The ascorbic acid content of different samples of the same food is known to vary enormously, and this is shown in the wide ranges (mashed potato analysed in meals-on-wheels 0·4–2·6 mg). For other details, turn to Table vi.

We also assayed some of the frequently served vegetables at intervals after cooking. There was, as expected, a considerable loss of the vitamin with keeping. For instance, a 100 g portion of boiled spring greens contained 6·7 mg ascorbic acid at 12 noon, but only one and a half hours later — by 1.30 p.m. — this had dropped to 3·7 mg ascorbic acid.

An example of the results of the low content of ascorbic acid in the delivered meals is shown in detail below as they affect one subject:

Subject No. 5
1st meals-on-wheels day (Monday)

Menu: 7 a.m. tea and biscuits
         8.15 a.m. boiled egg, brown bread and butter, tea
         12.30 p.m. delivered meal (espagnole steak, mashed potatoes, canned carrots, chocolate sultana sponge, custard)
         3 p.m. tea and biscuit
         5 p.m. ham, bread and butter, tea and biscuit
         9 p.m. coffee (made with all milk), cheese and biscuit, rum.

(a) Total *calculated* ascorbic acid (from Food Tables) for the whole day = 23 mg
(b) Total *calculated* ascorbic acid (from Food Tables) from delivered meal = 18 mg
(c) Therefore, total *calculated* ascorbic acid (from Food Tables) from rest of menu = 5 mg
(d) Total *analysed* ascorbic acid (duplicate sample of food *analysed at time of consumption*) from delivered meal = 0·9 mg
Note: (c) + (d) = 5·9 mg

It can be seen from the above example that this subject was consuming only 5·9 mg ascorbic acid on this day instead of the calculated 23 mg. (Food Tables figures indicated that most of the ascorbic acid came from the delivered meal and the rest from a moderate intake of milk in tea and coffee; our analysis showed this was not so.)

Fruit and Vegetables in the Weekly Diet

This day in the life of Subject No. 5 shows him eating no fruit or vegetables, other than the vegetables in the delivered meal. This was not uncommon: the diet records of 18 subjects who purchased only small quantities of fruits and vegetables were examined in detail and it was found that 15 of them did not eat their own purchases on the days meals-on-wheels were delivered. It seemed that they preferred to rely on meals-on-wheels for fruits and vegetables, reserving their own small supplies for the days when there was no delivered meal. However, over the whole week all our 100 subjects ate some fruits and vegetables in addition to those supplied in the delivered meals. Eleven who did not buy them for themselves were given them by friends or relatives.

Details of the main sources of ascorbic acid in the total diet during the survey weeks are given in Table vii (Appendix A, page

188). Fruits and vegetables, other than those shown in the table, e.g. apples, cucumbers, lettuces, beans, were eaten by some but these were not main sources of the vitamin. Purchases of frozen fruits and frozen vegetables were seldom made.

Table vii shows that for the majority, potatoes were the main source of ascorbic acid. They were served in meals-on-wheels and were also, generally, purchased for other days. They were eaten by all but one, and contributed a daily calculated average of 9 mg of the vitamin. After potatoes, the vegetables most eaten were cabbage or greens; 70 subjects ate them, but they provided them with an average of only 4 mg ascorbic acid a day.

Fruits were eaten less frequently and by fewer subjects; some of the fruits, but not all, contributed quite large amounts of vitamin C. Bananas were eaten by the greatest number (35) but provided them with an average of only 3 mg of the vitamin a day. Oranges came next in frequency; these were eaten by 20 people, and provided them with a daily average of 22 mg. The most potent source was canned blackcurrants, eaten by one subject, or blackcurrant syrup, taken by three subjects, and these provided over 60 mg as a daily average for these four people.

There were other fruits and vegetables served in meals-on-wheels, e.g. canned mixed vegetables, canned and fresh carrots and canned rhubarb, which contributed only between 0·4–0·9 mg daily, *far less ascorbic acid than the raw tomatoes and bananas bought by the old age pensioners themselves.*

Seasonal Variations
Although it is acknowledged that there is a decrease in average vitamin C intake during the winter months, the menu can over-ride this factor, e.g. two of the subjects studied in November had the

highest vitamin C intakes of the whole sample because their diet record included canned blackcurrants at the weekend, or a daily vitamin C blackcurrant drink.

Ascorbic Acid Intake of 100 Elderly Subjects

Having looked (Table vii) at the main pattern of consumption of fruits and vegetables, we are now in a better position to understand the ascorbic acid intakes of our elderly sample, as shown in Table 5.

Table 5
Ascorbic Acid Intake of 100 Elderly Subjects

Range of intake (mg/day)	Number of Subjects		
	m/w days	Other days	Whole week
0–29	68	40	47
30–59	21	43	37
60+	11	17	16

Mean intake (mg/day)	m/w days	Other days	Whole week
	28	41	37

It was not possible to analyse ascorbic acid in all the foods eaten by every subject on every day during the survey week. So the calculated (Food Tables) figure had to be used for foods other than meals-on-wheels. The intake figures in Table 5 are therefore a mixture of analysed values for delivered meals (which had ascorbic acid destruction due to long delays between cooking and consumption) and Food Tables values for other meals. This is probably more accurate than it may sound! Apart from meals-on-wheels, much of the ascorbic acid was provided by fresh fruit or tomatoes, moreover there was little evidence that the subjects cooked their meals long in advance or kept them hot before eating.

The results (Table 5) show that the average daily intake over the week was 37 mg; as many as 47% of the subjects were consuming less than the recommended intake of 30 mg. The mean intake on 'meals' days was much lower than on other days.

We have the paradoxical situation, therefore, that if it were decided to improve nutrition by an increase in the number of meals delivered, the ascorbic acid intake might be reduced and a greater proportion of the subjects could be receiving less than 30 mg a day.

Can Meals-on-Wheels Provide More Vitamin C?

The various suggestions that are made for an improvement in the ascorbic acid content of meals-on-wheels are discussed below:

Alterations in Timing, Preparation and Cooking Methods

To attempt to alter the timing, preparation or cooking methods of meals-on-wheels is not, under most circumstances, a very practical suggestion. In Portsmouth, the kitchen staff were already working extremely hard, and it would be difficult to see how they could produce varied meals in large numbers to be delivered over a wide area significantly nearer to the time of consumption. Nevertheless, some improvements might be possible. In one meals-on-wheels and luncheon club kitchen visited in Kensington, London, the supervisor had installed a machine to steam-cook vegetables in small batches under pressure. The elderly recipients were persuaded to accept just-cooked, instead of the usual very over-cooked vegetables, by first steam-cooking shredded cabbage under pressure for 2 minutes (over-cooked), then in the ensuing weeks cutting cooking time to the recommended 1½ minutes (now accepted by the diners). Rapid batch cooking like this enables vegetables to be cooked nearer to the time of collection by the meals-on-wheels van.

Even when kitchens cannot afford new equipment such as pressure steamers, some improvements might be made in large scale catering. For instance, in some of the institutions visited by the Gerontology Nutrition Unit, the most common observations of poor cooking practices were: potatoes peeled on the previous day, left soaking overnight, cooked and mashed long before serving time; green vegetables cut up the day prior to use, and the next day placed in cold water plus bicarbonate of soda and then boiled for over three quarters of an hour. Dried or canned processed peas were often used in place of canned garden or frozen peas, and in some instances were heated in the oven; likewise canned mixed vegetables, after being taken out of the tin, were washed off and heated dry in the oven for half an hour. Needless to say where this was practised only small quantities needed to be cooked due to the unpopularity of these 'bullets'.

However, unless the diner can be brought to the meal (luncheon club) rather than the meal to the diner (meals-on-wheels), the ascorbic acid benefits of improved cooking practices are diminished by the delays of delivery. Nevertheless, there is still a bonus with good cooking practices, of palatability and attractive appearance.

Changing the Menus

The variety of vegetables in the delivered meals could perhaps be increased. This might be desirable because one-quarter of our subjects said they would like to have more of a second vegetable. However, cooked vegetables provide very little ascorbic acid by the time a delivered meal is consumed. A major source of ascorbic acid in meals-on-wheels is the first vegetable, potatoes, but these in Portsmouth were already supplied in sufficient quantity. Almost half our subjects said the portion of potatoes in the delivered meals was over-generous, only two said they would like more, and some potato was wasted in 40 of the 200 meals.

An alternative to more cooked vegetables could be to serve some popular raw vegetables which would contribute vitamin C, e.g. tomatoes, and finely prepared coleslaw flavoured with lemon juice. Or possibly the use of continental recipes such as cabbage (green or red) cooked with apple in an acid medium, e.g. vinegar (which lessens destruction of vitamin C). Such cooked recipes are especially suitable for meals-on-wheels as the flavour is even enhanced with keeping; even so, it is advisable to introduce them first in small quantities until popularly accepted.

Provision of a Frozen Food Meal

Many authorities are finding that meals-on-wheels are readily acceptable and are easiest to provide when chosen from menus supplied by frozen food companies. Vegetables which are frozen within a short time of harvesting generally retain a higher proportion of vitamin C than vegetables which have spent hours travelling from garden to market to shop to kitchen. However, this does not necessarily mean that the provision of frozen vegetables in meals-on-wheels would improve their vitamin C content. Information is needed on the ascorbic acid content of frozen foods *under meals-on-wheels cooking and delivery conditions*. Even if frozen peas contribute more vitamin C than over-cooked cabbage, it is doubtful whether the higher levels would survive the long, warm delivery time and possible delays before consumption.

Microwave Cooking

There has been research into the feasibility of re-heating frozen meals rapidly, by microwave, in the van outside the house as each meal is delivered. This is said to produce a more attractive, palatable meal. In one experimental delivery round between 12 noon and 2 p.m. the meals are thus heated and straightaway delivered.

However, one would need to be sure that they are also straightaway eaten! In Portsmouth we found that when meals-on-wheels were delivered too early, i.e. before the recipient's customary mealtime, they were either kept hot or reheated. When they were delivered too late, some recipients had already eaten a snack to damp down appetite, and might then wait even longer before reheating and eating. Thus a microwave meal — unless coinciding with each recipient's customary lunch time — might be cooked or reheated *three times* (a) before freezing, (b) before delivery and (c) before eating. This would inevitably result in further destruction of vitamin C and folate. Thus for retention of vitamin C the effectiveness of microwave cooked meals-on-wheels depends on time of delivery coinciding with time of consumption.

Provision of Ascorbic Acid Tablets
Apart from the general principle that nutrients are best provided in food, it is uncertain whether, without supervision, the recipients would take ascorbic acid tablets regularly. They might also confuse them with other 'medicines' that they are taking. The extent of medication among the elderly patients in one London Group Practice has been described (Law and Chalmers, 1976). The authors state: 'A third of our patients took three or four drugs a day, but only the most ingenious had devised any method of laying out a supply of drugs.'

The possible side effects of 'megadoses' has already been referred to earlier in this chapter.

Use of Fortified Foods
We investigated the loss of the vitamin in a commercial dehydrated potato preparation that contained added ascorbic acid (vitamin C). Two samples analysed three hours after preparation (i.e. a normal time lag for Portsmouth meals-on-wheels) still contained 42 mg and 35 mg/100 g compared with the 90 mg or so at the time of preparation. The analysed value for ascorbic acid in the ordinary mashed potato prepared from boiled fresh potatoes which was served in Portsmouth (Table vi) ranged from 0·4–2·6 mg/100 g. Commercial fortified preparations are now on the market but many brands contain no added vitamin C so it is necessary to enquire from the manufacturer. The claim of added ascorbic acid is not always made on the label.

Inclusion of Vitamin C-rich Items as a Dessert
Although fresh fruit seemed to be quite popular with our subjects, it was never served in Portsmouth meals-on-wheels because it was felt preferable to serve puddings which they might not cook for themselves. But if the budget allows, vitamin C-rich fruits could be used; the DHSS Circular 5/70 suggested that a fresh orange should be prepared and served once a week. An alternative could be the serving of vitamin C-rich sauces.

Manufacturers might be persuaded to introduce a squeeze tube of blackcurrant purée, or a cheaper fruit-flavoured purée rich in ascorbic acid; these could help to increase ascorbic acid intake in the elderly (as well as in others whose diet is deficient in fruits and vegetables). A fruit purée would be a simple addition to breakfast cereals as well as to desserts. A squeeze tube which eliminates oxygen as it is flattened would overcome oxidation and consequent destruction of ascorbic acid.

Inclusion of Drinks Rich in Ascorbic Acid
It is an excellent idea, if funds permit, to serve refreshing orange juice or other cold drinks which are rich in ascorbic acid. An electric continuous juice separator could be used to make attractive fresh drinks from inexpensive raw vegetables and fruits. Small, individual non-spill containers might be needed because it is difficult to carry large jugs.

Luncheon Clubs
More people are being encouraged to visit luncheon clubs, where meals can be prepared with a shorter interval between cooking and serving. Perhaps for many elderly people who need assistance to get out, a combination of meals-on-wheels and luncheon clubs would be the most practicable.

Eating of Sweets
A number of elderly people eat sweets not just because they like them but because sucking a sweet takes away the dryness and 'bad taste' that sometimes results from taking medicines. Particularly if their diet is low in fruits and vegetables, it could be suggested that they suck sweets containing ascorbic acid, e.g. Boots (own brand) Blackcurrant Flavour Drops contain 5 mg vitamin C per sweet.

I never thought I would be advocating the eating of sweets — but this is an exception. And I still say 'after meals only' — not to spoil the appetite.

VITAMIN D

One of the main functions of vitamin D is to transport the strengthening material, calcium, to the bones. Deficiency may lead to painful bone disorders, and muscle weakness.

Vitamin D is obtained from:

   (a) Exposure to sunlight — by conversion of a precursor in the skin to vitamin D.

   (b) The diet — but there are only a limited number of foods containing reasonable amounts of this vitamin.

I never thought I would live to see the day when young girls got vitamin D in the places they do now!

The latest United Kingdom Recommended Daily Amounts Report (DHSS, 1979) stresses that the chief source of vitamin D is not the diet but the action of ultra-violet light on the skin. However, the report continues 'The amount of the vitamin obtained in this way varies with latitude and environmental conditions and cannot at present be assessed. It is difficult therefore to recommend an amount to be provided in the diet.'

The whole subject of vitamin D is still under much fascinating discussion and investigation. Among the factors considered important, with regard to sunlight, are not only latitude and environmental conditions, but also the angle of the sun when the skin is exposed to sunlight, the duration of exposure, the amount and condition of the skin exposed (including the possible atrophy of sebaceous glands with ageing), the time of day, the season of the year and the altitude.

Only a limited number of foods contain reasonable amounts of vitamin D, e.g. fatty fish, margarine, eggs, liver, fortified evaporated milk, butter and preparations such as Ovaltine.

The vitamin D found in foods is measured in micrograms (μg) cholecalciferol or in i.u. (International Units) of vitamin D.

The latest DHSS (1979) recommendations further state:

> ... the intake of vitamin D from food or from vitamin supplements is a safeguard when exposure to sunlight is insufficient for the synthesis of enough vitamin D for health.

There is a footnote to this recommendation:

Adults with inadequate exposure to sunlight, for example those who are housebound, may need a supplement of 10μg daily.

It must be stressed that of our 100 meals-on-wheels recipients, 77 were of limited mobility, including one who was bedridden. Of these 77, 68 did not get out of doors to shop for food but had others to do their shopping for them.

As the vitamin D contribution from sunlight was therefore low for many of our meals-on-wheels recipients, their dietary vitamin D is now more closely examined. At the time of our survey, the DHSS (1969) recommended daily intake (RDI) was 2·5 μg cholecalciferol. But the new recommendation for adults, with inadequate exposure to sunlight, is now four times that amount: 10 μg daily.

Dietary Vitamin D Intakes of Some Elderly Groups

When comparing our (QEC) figures to the Government (DHSS) figures for dietary intake of vitamin D as shown in Table 6 below, in all cases the QEC figures were not only lower but were also well below the RDI at the time of the survey.

Table 6
A Comparison of Vitamin D Intake in Two Surveys
(μg Cholecalciferol)

	QEC[1]	DHSS[2] (all areas)	DHSS[3] (Portsmouth)
Men			
65–74 years	1·9	3·3	3·6
75 and over	2·1	2·7	3·1
Women			
65–74 years	1·8	2·3	2·0
75 and over	1·4	2·1	2·5

RDI = 2·5 μg
1 = QEC: Queen Elizabeth College, Gerontology Nutrition Unit, present report.
2 = DHSS: A Nutrition Survey of the Elderly, Rep.Hlth.Soc.Subj. No. 3. Department of Health and Social Security, pp.95–96.
3 = as above, pp.95–96.

In the DHSS Report, separate figures were given for the six different areas included in their survey. As Portsmouth was one of these areas, we were able to make a direct comparison with our Portsmouth sample. In the DHSS Report, vitamin D intake figures for Portsmouth were generally *higher* than in the other areas they surveyed; this makes our even lower figures for meals-on-wheels recipients a particular cause for concern.

When recording the diets of women aged 70 years and over, Exton-Smith and Stanton (1965) reported an average daily intake of 3·4 µg cholecalciferol (135 i.u. vit.D). But the ranges of intake were wide: 0·3–8·8 µg cholecalciferol (10–353 i.u. vit.D) per day.

The elderly who are housebound, as well as lacking exposure to sunlight, often have very low dietary intakes. This was illustrated by Exton-Smith and his colleagues (1972) who found that 48% of housebound women aged 70–79 years had a daily vitamin D intake of less than 0·75 µg (30 i.u.) compared with 13% of a similar age group of active women.

Lack of sunlight plus low intake of vitamin D equals poor vitamin D status.

Another category of the elderly found to have low dietary vitamin D intakes were patients in long-stay geriatric wards. Corless and his colleagues (1975) reported an average vitamin D content of a geriatric ward diet as only about 1·2 µg cholecalciferol per day (even lower than our meals-on-wheels group).

It is worth re-emphasising that the main food sources of vitamin D are limited. But luckily vitamin D (unlike vitamin C) is not easily destroyed by poor cooking practices.

There are many simple recipes contributing vitamin D together with calcium (Davies, 1972; 1979).

Unfortunately many of the vitamin D foods are unpopular with some elderly people. They may be afraid of the bones in fatty fish, some of them say they find eggs 'binding', or liver too strong in flavour. Margarine used to be a 'poor relation' of butter and is still considered socially inferior by many of the older generation, although this trend may be changing. (Margarine which is fortified with vitamin D is a far richer source than butter.)

Our ten subjects with the lowest vitamin D intakes (0·3–0·5 µg/ day) ate no fatty fish or margarine, and only small quantities of butter, eggs and other vitamin D foods. The ten with the highest vitamin D intakes (4·2–8·7 µg/day) had a diet noticeably higher in fatty fish, eggs and butter although even these subjects ate no margarine. As mentioned earlier, in Chapter 6, the subject with the highest vitamin D intake had, in fact, been eating foods low in vitamin D but was taking a supplement of Glucodin, a glucose product enriched with the vitamin.

The table below shows the dietary intake of vitamin D on the two days on which meals-on-wheels were delivered (m/w days) compared with the other weekdays when there were no delivered meals. It shows the low contribution of vitamin D from the delivered meals-on-wheels.

Table 7
Dietary Intake of Vitamin D From Meals-on-Wheels (m/w)
(μg Cholecalciferol)

	Contribution from the delivered meal	Daily intake on m/w days	Daily intake on other weekdays
mean	0·4	1·8	1·9
range	0·0–1·6	0·3–15·0	0·1–12·9

There was no marked difference in the mean dietary vitamin D intake between m/w days and other weekdays. The 200 meals delivered to our 100 subjects were low in vitamin D, six meals containing none.

Vitamin D deficiency leads to osteomalacia and may also in part be responsible for the development of osteoporosis: these are two bone disorders common in the elderly which cause pain and often muscular weakness. They may also result in deformity or bone fractures.

Professor Exton-Smith and his colleagues (1972) in their report on the nutrition of housebound old people stated that the six who had sustained fractures of the femur had a considerably lower mean dietary vitamin D intake than that for the whole housebound group. The case histories of our meals-on-wheels survey were therefore examined and it was found that the mean dietary vitamin D intake for our 13 subjects who had sustained bone fractures (unspecified) was 1·1 μg compared with the mean of the whole group of 1·7 μg, a 35% decrease.

Exton-Smith (1970) considers that there is also evidence that the liability to osteoporosis in the elderly is determined at least in part by the skeletal development before maturity. So past exposure to sunlight and past nutrition is of importance; but so is present nutrition.

There are a few conditions in which medicinal supplementation may be necessary, e.g. for osteomalacia, in some renal disorders, where there is malabsorption or where the use of drugs such as anticonvulsants alter vitamin D metabolism. But these are conditions which call for long-term measures and carefully controlled dosage with close medical supervision because of the danger of toxicity.

For the majority gentler measures should suffice. We should first ask an important question: *could some who are at present considered housebound be persuaded to seek the sunlight*? Some recommendations are listed below:

- Sunlight should not be confused with overpowering exposure to hot sunshine: just pushing back sleeves and opening a collar in pleasant daylight can be beneficial.
- Even the frailest of residents in old people's homes may enjoy afternoon tea temptingly laid in a sheltered spot in the garden.
- Some 'non-shoppers' stay indoors mainly because they are afraid to venture out on their own, possibly for fear of being stranded if unwell. But many would enjoy being accompanied out to the shops occasionally, and having parcels carried home for them.
- Home Helps could be encouraged to position their house-bound or bed-ridden clients, even for a short period, in a shaft of sunlight coming through an open window.
- Volunteers helping an elderly neighbour with an outside chore such as gardening or hanging washing could also encourage them to participate or even just come outside to watch.
- Getting out to a luncheon club can merely mean exchanging one enclosed room for another so where possible some benches or chairs could be placed out of doors.
- A housebound state can be the result of living in a high rise building, or even being unable to negotiate one small flight of steps. For these so-called housebound, purpose-built housing should aim to bring easy access to the outside world.
- The hospital wards which have balconies, verandahs or access to gardens could be allocated to long stay patients so even the

bedridden could be wheeled out for periods into sunlit fresh air.

- It might be feasible to fit a special glass in some geriatric wards to allow the passage of ultra-violet light.
- For some patients the possibility of sunlamp treatment could also be considered.

The next question to consider is: *Must it be taken for granted that an increased dietary vitamin D intake is difficult to achieve?* For many it is because, as the cartoon at the beginning of this chapter has shown, the main sources are limited. Moreover (a sad commentary on modern diet) where are the cheap herrings, kippers, bloaters, mackerel and jellied eels? Expensive now because of over-fishing but nutritionally still to be recommended as superb value for money. Other fish which are excellent sources are sardines, tuna, pilchards, salmon, and cod roe. Where canning or sousing has softened the bones these can be eaten so that the calcium is utilised together with the vitamin D. Unfortunately bones and a distinctive flavour often make these fatty fish either unpopular or not acceptable as an 'everyday' food.

An alternative way to increase dietary vitamin D is to fortify foods. The DHSS (1972) report recommended prophylactic trials with vitamin D to see whether osteomalacia could be prevented in those patients considered by the GP to be 'at risk'. If osteomalacia persists in the community the report recommended possible fortification of milk with vitamin D. But so far these steps have not been implemented. It would be interesting to make comparisons with the USA where such a milk fortification programme exists. What have been the long term effects? These should surely be considered before a fortification programme is implemented in Britain. A logical extension to a fortification programme on a limited number of foods might be to add vitamin D to the dehydrated potato often used in luncheon clubs and meals-on-wheels, or to supplement with vitamin D the yoghurts served in these meals.

Other 'gentle means' to increase vitamin D intake from meals-on-wheels and similar large scale catering include, most importantly, greater use of margarine fortified with vitamin D (if fortification is not mentioned on the carton a check should be made with the supplier). In hospitals or other establishments where individual portions are served, manufacturers could produce small wrapped pats of fortified margarine.

Fishcakes and fish pies may be popular and some cooks in residential homes are already using recipes incorporating canned pilchards or mackerel instead of white fish. Kipper fillets used for making patés eliminate the scare of choking on bones. A proportion of finely chopped liver can be added to minced meat for dishes such as meat loaf and beefburgers, or meat sauces.

If measures such as these can improve vitamin D status i.e. by *increased* exposure to sunlight and *increased* dietary intake of vitamin D, it may be possible to avoid widespread supplementation. The long term effects of vitamin D dosage are not known and many of the elderly housebound could be receiving such dosages for twenty years or more. There are over threequarters of a million housebound elderly in the UK, and in my opinion many are already over-medicated. Although vitamin D dosage as prescribed would be well below the normal toxic level, some elderly patients may increase usage in a misguided attempt to find dramatic relief from pain; or they may confuse their medications.

It is virtually impossible to overdose on vitamin D from natural foods. Recorded cases are limited to such oddities as hearty meals of polar bear liver or the liver from a large halibut (that would be the food equivalent to an overdose of halibut liver oil).

The danger of excess vitamin D when consuming fortified foods is limited by one's appetite. It would be difficult to consume pounds of margarine and pints of fortified milk at a sitting. However fortification levels need to remain carefully controlled and any programme limited to only a few foods.

Guide to some Vitamin D Foods (μg/100g)

Herring/bloater (grilled)	25·0	Margarine	7·0–8·8
Kipper (baked)	25·0	Butter	0·7
Mackerel (fried)	21·1	Eggs	1·7
Canned salmon	12·5	Ox liver	1·1
Pilchards	8·0	Chicken liver	0·2
Sardines	7·5	Horlicks	1·5
Tuna	5·8	Ovaltine	8·3*
Cod roe (fried)	2·2	Fortified evap. milk	2·8*
		Grapenuts	3·5*

(From: Paul and Southgate, *The Composition of Foods*, 1978)
* Data supplied by manufacturers.

POTASSIUM

It was Professor Sir W. Ferguson Anderson who first suggested that, during the course of our meals-on-wheels survey, we might investigate the possible link between potassium intake and depression. He kindly obtained for us a copy of the Food Tables based on McCance and Widdowson (1960). These included some extra foods and recipes, which had already been added to the DHSS Food Composition Tables (1969).

As all Food Tables figures can only give an average from a few samples, we agreed that some analysis of the foods most commonly served in the Portsmouth meals-on-wheels would be of interest. It might be that modern use of fertilisers, or some other factor, would show up wide discrepancies, but in the event — as we shall see — our analyses showed close agreement with the Food Tables figures.

High Potassium Foods

Most foods contain moderate amounts of potassium (K) so there should be no shortage of this essential mineral in the average UK diet.

Low Potassium Foods

Foods which are very low in potassium include sugar and boiled sweets, marmalade, honey, butter and margarine, tea and proprietary squashes.

There is no internationally accepted recommendation for potassium, and textbooks on human nutrition give wide variations. Most dietary intakes provide from 50–150 mmol (2·0–5·8 g) potassium a day; the 'normal' figure for the population in general is about 65 mmol (2·5 g) per day (Davidson *et al.*, 1979).

Fig.2

DIETARY POTASSIUM INTAKE: NUMBER OF SUBJECTS IN EACH INTAKE GROUP
Intake in M Eq

Intake	Number of subjects
20–29	1 (number of subjects)
30–39	10
40–49	21
50–59	37
60–69	22
70–79	4
80–89	3
90–99	–
100-109	2

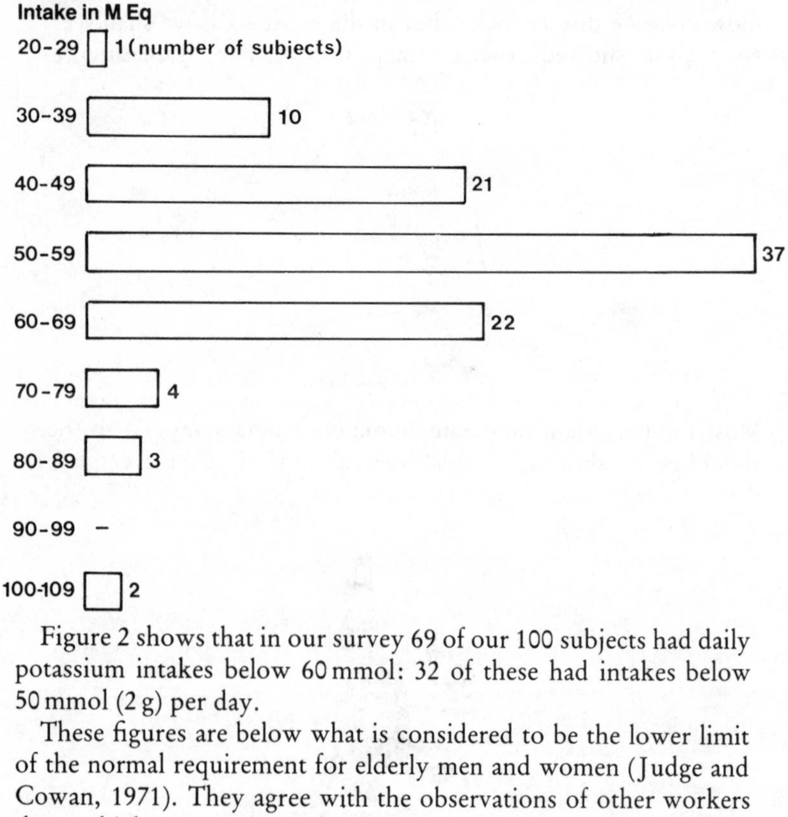

Figure 2 shows that in our survey 69 of our 100 subjects had daily potassium intakes below 60 mmol: 32 of these had intakes below 50 mmol (2 g) per day.

These figures are below what is considered to be the lower limit of the normal requirement for elderly men and women (Judge and Cowan, 1971). They agree with the observations of other workers that a high proportion of elderly people select a diet low in potassium.

Fig.3

**DIETARY POTASSIUM INTAKE: AGE AND SEX
(AVERAGE DAILY INTAKE FOR WHOLE WEEK)**

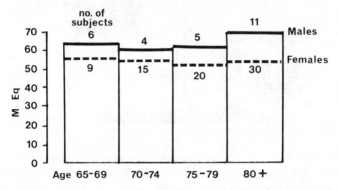

The figure above shows that the men in our survey had a higher mean dietary potassium intake than the women. But this needs to be interpreted further: it is important to realise that it is possible to have an inadequate potassium dietary intake either from foods low in potassium or from a low food intake.

The men had a higher energy intake than the women: when we calculated the average potassium intake per 1000 kcal, it was similar for men (29·5 mmol potassium/1000 kcal) and women (30·0 mmol potassium/1000 kcal). So, in spite of the higher potassium intakes shown in Figure 3, the men were not choosing foods higher in potassium than were the women — they were just, on average, eating more.

Potassium intake did not necessarily fall with advancing age, and this also is shown in Figure 3.

The two delivered meals, although providing an average of 28 mmol (1·1 g) potassium per meal only slightly increased the daily potassium intake; the average daily intake for the whole week was 55 mmol (range 28–108 mmol). The average intake on meals-on-wheels days was 58 mmol, on other weekdays 53 mmol and at weekends 55 mmol.

Analyses

Different samples of the same food can vary widely in potassium content, even when bought in the same locality and cooked in the same kitchen. As already stated some of the foods most commonly

eaten in the Portsmouth meals-on-wheels were analysed for potassium (for method see page 49). Table viii (Appendix A), shows that our analysed values agreed closely with the tables based on McCance and Widdowson (1960) for meat, fish and dairy foods but, for reasons explained in the footnote to Table viii, varied considerably for fruit and vegetables.

Deficiency of potassium is associated with muscle weakness, including poor grip strength, and Judge and Cowan (1971) point out that it may therefore be incorrect to regard such weakness as exclusively a part of physiological ageing. Potassium depletion has also been associated with mental confusion, depression and under-nutrition (Fowlie et al., 1963; Dall and Gardiner, 1971).

We asked our investigators to record in each case study their subjective assessment of a state of depression. This was not a medical diagnosis, but they were in close contact with each subject.

An example of one of the case studies which led to an assessment of depression is given below:

> *Subject 85*   Female aged 72. At the time of asking for meals-on-wheels had phlebitis and ulcerated legs. Legs now healed. Had a fall a month ago. Takes 6 iron jelloids daily. Husband died two years ago, still tearful about it. Husband was 'such a good old stick', her zest has gone. Has two sons, one who visits infrequently. No old friends except one neighbour who visits weekly to go for a walk. Disconsolate at deterioration of house. Apathetic about cooking and eating. Sometimes meals-on-wheels are her only two cooked meals in the week.

Of the 7 subjects on a very low potassium intake (less than 38 mmol per day), four had been assessed as being depressed. One, not assessed as depressed, was in fact receiving extra potassium through medication. The assessments were 'blind', i.e. the investigator did not know the dietary potassium intake (Table ix).

Of the total 100 subjects in the survey, 35 were considered to be lonely and depressed. There was a significant relationship between potassium intake and assessment of depression ($\chi^2 = 13.916$, $p < 0.001$). The mean daily potassium intake of the 35 'depressed' was lower than that of the 65 'not depressed', and this was associated with a lower energy intake (for details, see Table ix Appendix A, page 190).

It must be emphasised, however, that there is no clear-cut picture. *Ranges* of potassium intakes, rather than the *average*, were similar for the 'depressed' and 'non-depressed'. Moreover, which comes first? Does depression cause some — though not all — subjects to lose their appetite or to turn to an easy, high sugar diet, resulting in potassium depletion? Or does potassium depletion, coupled with a low energy intake, lead to depression? These are questions still to be investigated.

Judge (1968) found that the most common association of hypoka-
laemia (low serum potassium) in the elderly was a recent cerebrovascular accident (stroke) or the use of oral diuretics. Thirty four of
our subjects had suffered some form of cerebrovascular disease (this
might have been the reason for them receiving meals-on-wheels)
and 14 had a prescription for an oral diuretic.

An oral diuretic increases the output of sodium and water in the
urine, but it also increases potassium excretion. Dall, Paulose and
Fergusson (1971) showed that when elderly patients were given an
oral diuretic they readily became hypokalaemic and needed a
minimum daily supplement of 24 mmol potassium for replacement
therapy. Unfortunately, some potassium supplements induce ulceration of the small intestine. So again we have the message: medical
doses of nutrients must be prescribed with the utmost care.

But what of those elderly men and women without drastic
symptoms, e.g. the many subjects who were reported by our four
investigators as showing 'a marked lack of interest in food'. We
have seen that many of the elderly subjects in our survey had a low
dietary potassium intake. It would therefore seem advisable for
health visitors, and other visitors, who notice a small appetite,
apathy, depression and general disinterest in food to advise simple
steps which would increase potassium intake from foods. It is
useless to try to increase the appetite of a depressed, weak, confused
or apathetic old lady by urging her to cook a nourishing casserole.
In fact, two-thirds of the 'depressed' subjects in our survey even
wasted part of the meals-on-wheels which were delivered to them
ready-cooked.

What is needed under these circumstances is easy-to-follow

dietary advice not calling for a great deal of effort in shopping, preparation, cooking or eating.

- Our findings agree with those of Judge and Macleod (1968) who advise a pint of milk each day, providing 23·5 mmol (0·9 g) potassium. For instance, instead of the inevitable cups of sweetened tea, there could be persuasion to take the occasional milky drink such as milky coffee, providing approximately 10 mmol (0·4 g) potassium per cup, a milky chocolate drink providing approximately 8 mmol (0·3 g) potassium per cup, or Marmite made with milk providing approximately 12 mmol (0·5 g) potassium per cup (some like this as a savoury drink, others serve it as a quick soup). Some other commercial 'nightcap' preparations are also rich in potassium and are used at the rate of about 1 or 2 teaspoons per cup of milk.

- There should be encouragement to eat easily prepared (sometimes ready-to-eat) snacks. Of our 100 subjects, 23% were sometimes eating 'nothing' between lunch and the following day's breakfast. 'Nothing' has been defined as merely a beverage, sometimes with biscuit or plain bread and butter; this is taken as a sign of apathy towards food preparation and would be a contributory cause of low potassium intake.

- Suggestions for snacks and very simple recipe ideas for 'non-cooks' are given in *Easy Cooking for One or Two* and *More Easy Cooking for One or Two*, books written particularly for the elderly, (Davies, 1972; 1979), A non-cook is defined not only as someone who cannot cook, but also those who are too tired or ill to bother. Recipes such as 'Bread and Milk' and 'Lazy Soup' (made with Marmite) were among those included to increase potassium intake. However, for those requiring a low sodium intake, there are also high potassium/low sodium recipes utilizing fruits.

- An easily stocked 'Emergency Food Store' cupboard could also encourage an interest in food, especially on days when shopping is not possible. Suggestions, with a shopping check list, are given in a cartoon slide nutrition education lecture kit, produced for the elderly and those looking after them (Gerontology Nutrition Unit, 1973–5.)

- If even easy snacks are too much bother, the provision of orange juice with meals-on-wheels would contribute not only vitamin C but also about 5 mmol (0·2 g) potassium in a small glass.

- There could be a recommendation for bananas, which we found popular with many old people. A banana is easy to peel and eat and even a small one provides about 5 mmol (0·2 g) potassium.

- It is of interest that cornflakes are far lower in potassium than most other breakfast cereals, yet cornflakes were, in our survey, the most commonly eaten cereal. Other cereals such as All Bran, Bemax, Grapenuts and Puffed Wheat — eaten with milk and possibly sweetened with sultanas or other fruit instead of sugar — are to be encouraged as a simple means of improving potassium intake.

ENERGY

The body obtains the energy it requires from foods and beverages containing carbohydrate (starches and sugars), protein, fat and, for those who consume it, alcohol.

In lectures to the elderly and those looking after them the Gerontology Nutrition Unit uses simple cartoons to explain why energy in needed.

Physical movement and exercise

Food also provides energy for basal metabolism, i.e. for the less obvious normal life processes such as heart beat and circulation and, as illustrated above, maintenance of internal warmth.

Appetite and Energy Intake

It has so frequently been said 'Of course, old people eat less as they grow older' that I almost began to doubt the evidence of my own eyes: the many old men and women I had seen tucking into hearty meals. What has caused this belief that it is *old age itself* that brings diminished appetite, i.e. diminished energy intake?

It is true that FAO/WHO (1973) recommend a progressive decrease in energy intake for the older age groups. Their recommendations for energy intake with advancing age are based on the assumptions that there will be (a) a change in body weight or body composition; (b) a decrease in basal metabolic rate; (c) a decline in physical activity; and (d) an increased prevalence of diseases and disabilities.

Certainly it is recognised that there is a loss of lean body mass (body composition excluding adipose tissue) from the age of 25 onwards (Shock, 1972). Likewise there is a fall in basal metabolism. Durnin and Passmore (1967) estimate that by the age of 80 the resting metabolism will have fallen to about 85% of the value at 25 years. However they point out that this decline will reduce the energy expenditure of an octogenarian by only about 200 kcal/day.

Energy expenditure is more importantly reduced by a reduction in physical activity, but even when physical activities are similar in the same age group, energy expenditure varies. Durnin and his colleagues (1966) found that one elderly farmer could expend twice as much energy as another, even though they were engaged in the same occupation.

Requirements of individuals can vary greatly — from one extreme to another it can vary as much as fivefold.

Many disabilities and diseases reduce energy intake and expenditure, but there are some exceptions: an even larger energy expenditure than normal has been reported in the efforts of dealing with disabilities such as hemiplegia or deformation of bones. In other words a reduction in physical activity is the main cause of reduced energy requirements so when, in old age, physical activity is maintained it should never be taken for granted that age alone will cause a marked reduction in energy requirements in that individual.

It is undoubtedly true that most middle-aged and elderly people (and many young ones too) would rather watch a tennis match on television than participate, but the 1981 London Marathon was not without its octogenarian competitor!

Not many old people are as active as he, or as the centenarian shepherd interviewed in the Caucasus and depicted in our cartoon (Leaf 1973). However they are not unique. Durnin and Passmore (1967) cite the energy expenditure of a man of 80 (one of the active farmers studied) as being 3140 kcal/day. There were a number of physically active elderly people in our survey sample.

In contrast, there are elderly men and women crippled, say, with arthritis who, in spite of their severely diminished physical activity, still retain a powerful appetite and yet do not become obese. Energy requirements — as we have said — vary greatly according to the individual.

Where weight is maintained without undue losses or gains, the energy content of the diet can be taken to be satisfactory. When the total energy intake is markedly inadequate, protein will be used for energy purposes with an accompanying loss of lean body tissue. Unexpected weight changes — either marked losses or gains — may be due to a decline in health or emotional state and therefore need to be investigated.

Energy Intakes in the Survey

In this chapter, when interpreting our survey data, it is essential to remember that the recommended daily intake (RDI) for energy (DHSS 1969) relates only to *groups* of the population and is simply

Fig.4

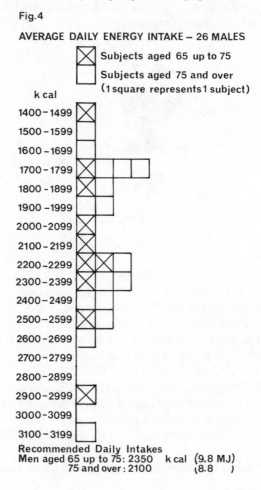

AVERAGE DAILY ENERGY INTAKE – 26 MALES

☒ Subjects aged 65 up to 75

☐ Subjects aged 75 and over
(1 square represents 1 subject)

Recommended Daily Intakes
Men aged 65 up to 75: 2350   k cal (9.8 MJ)
         75 and over : 2100   (8.8   )

an estimated *average* requirement, with some individuals requiring more and some less.

(For other nutrients, the RDI is based not on average requirements but on the amount sufficient, or more than sufficient, for the nutritional needs of practically all healthy persons in that group of the population. So the RDI for these other nutrients is probably in excess of the needs of most.)

Fig.5

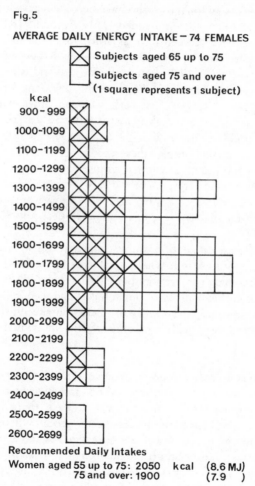

AVERAGE DAILY ENERGY INTAKE — 74 FEMALES

☒ Subjects aged 65 up to 75

☐ Subjects aged 75 and over
(1 square represents 1 subject)

Recommended Daily Intakes
Women aged 55 up to 75: 2050   kcal   (8.6 MJ)
          75 and over: 1900   (7.9)

Our sample was divided into *groups* according to age and sex. Figures 4 and 5 illustrate the wide ranges of individual intakes within the groups. Table iv, Appendix A, p. 186 records that as a group, only the older males had an average energy intake equal to the RDI; in other groups, the average energy intake was lower than the recommendations.

This could point to under-nutrition in the groups, with some individuals losing weight and/or reducing activity. Or it could be that the 1969 RDIs for energy for elderly groups were pitched too high, particularly for those who have become markedly inactive.

In fact the new Recommended Daily Amounts (RDA) (DHSS, 1979) for elderly women have assumed just this; the new recommendation for women aged 55 up to 75 years has been reduced from the original (DHSS 1969) figure of 2050 kcal and is now 1900 kcal. Similarly, for women aged 75 years and over, the RDA has been reduced from 1900 to 1680 kcal. On the other hand the new recommendations very slightly increase (by 50 kcal) the recommendations for elderly men.

In terms of our sample. these recommendations mean that the older men and the older women would now be considered to meet the RDA (intakes, respectively 100% and 104% of the RDA); however the men and women aged 65–74 years are still below the new recommendations (average intakes respectively 90% and 84% of the RDA).

In the Potassium section of this chapter it was stressed that many of our elderly meals-on-wheels recipients had a small appetite and showed marked disinterest in food. We have just illustrated (Figures 4 and 5) that the majority of our subjects had seemingly low energy intakes. However, the *ranges* of energy intake illustrated in our survey were very wide — some of our individuals had hearty appetites.

In our sample there were 65 women and 20 men over 70 years of age. Figures 6 and 7 show there was no marked drop in mean energy intake between the 70s and the 80s. Indeed, there was an actual increase for women in the successive age groups: there was interest in food among men and women in the late 70s and 80+ groups.

In contrast, Exton-Smith and Stanton (1965) had reported a fall in energy and nutrient intakes from the early to the late 70s. These subjects were elderly women living alone and mostly not receiving meals-on-wheels. In a longitudinal* study (Stanton and Exton-

Fig. 6

AVERAGE DAILY ENERGY INTAKE: AGE AND SEX

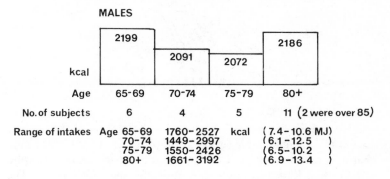

MALES

kcal	2199	2091	2072	2186
Age	65-69	70-74	75-79	80+
No. of subjects	6	4	5	11 (2 were over 85)

Range of intakes	Age 65-69	1760-2527	kcal	(7.4-10.6 MJ)
	70-74	1449-2997		(6.1-12.5)
	75-79	1550-2426		(6.5-10.2)
	80+	1661-3192		(6.9-13.4)

Fig. 7

AVERAGE DAILY ENERGY INTAKE; AGE AND SEX

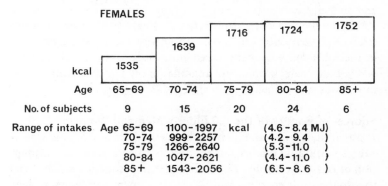

FEMALES

kcal	1535	1639	1716	1724	1752
Age	65-69	70-74	75-79	80-84	85+
No. of subjects	9	15	20	24	6

Range of intakes	Age 65-69	1100-1997	kcal	(4.6-8.4 MJ)
	70-74	999-2257		(4.2-9.4)
	75-79	1266-2640		(5.3-11.0)
	80-84	1047-2621		(4.4-11.0)
	85+	1543-2056		(6.5-8.6)

Smith, 1970) they investigated this further and stated that 'the falls in intakes during the eighth decade revealed by the cross-sectional study (of 1965) probably do not represent true age changes; rather we would refer to them as age differences which can be accounted for by the consequences of increasing physical and mental disabilities which afflict a large proportion of people during this decade.' A decline in nutrient intake, they said, can be attributed to disease rather than to age alone.

* For definitions see footnote to p. 11

A study of our sample seems to support this view: it was found that men and women with the lowest appetite included those who were feeble, both physically and mentally, *regardless of age.* The subjects in the 80+ age range who had higher daily energy intakes were mentally active, were interested in food, and were making the most of their physical capabilities. Whether they were physically and mentally active because they ate more food, or whether a higher energy intake allowed greater activity cannot be assessed from this study. Ten years after our survey, seven very elderly survivors (now in their 80s and 90s) were traced and, as discussed in Chapter 11, when they were keeping to a similar meal pattern, their energy intake was maintained *in spite of deteriorating health.*

Sources of Energy of the 100 Elderly Men and Women
It might be wondered whether a high energy intake among elderly subjects could be due to a 'lazy' diet, with an increased consumption of fats and carbohydrates. However, investigation showed that the sources of energy of these elderly men and women were generally similar to those for younger individuals.

A comparison was made with households with one man and one woman both under 55 years, as shown in the National Food Survey figures for 1970 (Ministry of Agriculture, Fisheries and Food, 1973). These comparative figures are shown in brackets. The energy supplied by protein, fats and carbohydrate respectively was 12% (11·7%), 40% (43·8%) and 48% (44·5%) of the total. However, in the present survey the range was wide: 9–21% energy came from protein, 27–49% energy came from fat and 32–63% energy came from carbohydrate. In other words, there were wide individual variations.

Energy Provided by Meals-on-Wheels
— Some Facts and Figures

- On average, energy intakes rose on days when meals-on-wheels were delivered. They were slightly lower at weekends than during the rest of the week. (For fuller details see Table x, Appendix A, page 191.)

- On average, the delivered meal provided 38% of the mean RDI for energy. This is slightly more than the average amount eaten during the lunch period by the elderly participants (who were mostly not receiving meals-on-wheels) in the Nutrition Survey of the Elderly (DHSS 1972).

- The average Portsmouth delivered meal with no wastage supplied 830 kcal (3·5 MJ); range 400–1170 kcal (1·7–4·9 MJ).

- Of the 200 meals served, there was wastage in 62 (largely potato, sometimes meat or dessert). The recipients of these 62 meals consumed on average 615 kcal (2·6 MJ).

- The mean energy intake from all the meals-on-wheels was therefore 760 kcal (range 190–1170) or 3·2 MJ (range 0·8–4·9).

- Of the 16 meals providing less than 500 kcal (2·1 MJ) wastage had occured in 15.

- Another 16 meals provided more than 1000 kcal (4·2 MJ). This was due to an unusually large portion of one or more of the dishes and/or a carbohydrate-rich dish, such as pie or pudding. For example, in one meal providing 1080 kcal (4·5 MJ) over 12 oz cottage pie had been served followed by 4 oz chocolate and sultana pudding with 5 oz chocolate sauce.

Reasons for Lack of Energy Benefit from Meals-on-Wheels

Although the recommendations for energy are admittedly based on inadequate evidence and their further revision may be desirable, it was still thought to be of interest at the time of the survey to express daily energy intakes as a percentage of the 1969 RDIs.

There were 31 subjects with an average daily energy intake below 80% of the RDI. Of these, 14 ate at least 200 kcal (0·8 MJ) more than usual on meals-on-wheels days. The diet of the other 17 remained practically unaltered by the delivered meal and these 17 cases were studied in detail.

There was wastage of food in 21 of the 34 meals received by these 17 (like all the subjects they were receiving two meals-on-wheels per week). The case histories of these subjects showed one or more of the following factors: a lack of interest in food; a small appetite; physical incapacity; illness; slimming; dental trouble; loneliness; nervous state and embittered personality. It is, of course, possible that the small food intakes could have been due to an individual energy requirement less than 80% of the RDI, particularly because so many of our subjects were of limited mobility.

It is obviously important not to assume that the provision of meals-on-wheels will automatically increase the food intake in subjects who are neglecting their diet.

Evans and Stock (1972) have shown that in two geriatric wards there was an 18% difference in energy and nutrient intake in the ward where there was assistance with feeding from nursing staff, compared with the adjacent ward where the staff could not give as much help.

Where there are physical and psychological difficulties which affect food intake (as shown in the 17% of our sample reported above) prompt and positive remedial help may be needed to augment the provision of meals-on-wheels. The type of help envisaged could include a few meals taken in company at luncheon clubs or day centres, good neighbour visits, help with feeding, or some simple cooking or shopping assistance.

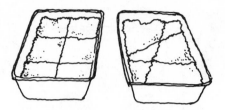

Portion Control

The delivered meals supplied anything from 400 to 1170 kcal. Although this was partly due to the menu, it was probably also attributable to lack of experience in portion control. Incidentally, the sizes of meals were *not* intentionally adjusted to suit the estimated appetites of the recipients: they were intended to be approximately the same.

The need for portion control to avoid unnecessary wastage and to ensure fair distribution of nutrients should be stressed in all institutions and to all organisations providing meals. They need all the mechanical help available, e.g. scoops, practice in cutting straight lines or even occasionally the placing of plates on scales so that approximate weights can be seen. There may in fact be a case for giving some small and some large portions according to appetite if the meals are clearly labelled for each recipient. One woman actually stopped taking meals-on-wheels because her husband had such a small appetite that she felt it was a waste of money to pay for the large portions delivered. It would not be feasible to have two prices according to size, because this might lead to under-eating in order to economise. It would be better, if there were sufficient liaison between the kitchen and the meals-on-wheels deliverers, to have some meals marked as extra-small or extra-large portions. Failing this, in some areas, extra-hungry clients are unofficially 'slipped' two meals, especially if there is one left over at the end of the round.

PROTEIN

In our lectures to the elderly and those looking after them the cartoons we use show that protein is the main material for building and repairing the body — that includes muscles, bones, nerves, blood, vital organs, hair and finger nails. We stress that even when

adults are fully grown or ageing, protein building is essential as all parts of the body are continually breaking down and having to be replaced.

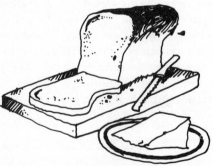

A wide variety of protein-rich foods and therefore amino acids (protein constituents) were being eaten by the elderly men and women participating in our survey. They included the animal protein-rich foods, e.g. meat, poultry, fish, eggs, cheese and milk;

also the main vegetable protein-rich foods, e.g. bread and other cereal foods, peas, beans and lentils. In strict vegetarian diets, when vegetable proteins alone are eaten, it is important to include both cereals (e.g. breads, rice) and pulses (e.g. beans, lentils) so all the essential amino acids are obtained. Likewise a small amount of protein from animal sources, for example milk or eggs added to such a diet, will improve the protein quality.

Many of our subjects were obtaining protein from mixed animal and vegetable sources. This was often due to a choice of traditional dishes (enjoyed instinctively by our ancestors long before the science of nutrition gave its seal of approval), such as roast beef and Yorkshire pudding, fish and chips, bread and cheese, porridge and milk.

Bodies — like cars — don't always run smoothly.

In the UK, which has bread (an important source of protein) as its staple food, and a wide supply of other protein-rich foods, it is rare for anyone to go short of protein. However, sometimes things go wrong, and the body needs extra protein. There were a number of our subjects who at some periods may have needed some *extra* protein, for example:

- During convalescence after operations, or with fever, fractures, burns or pressure sores.
- When extra flesh was needed to be put back on wasted bodies,

e.g. following self neglect or semi-starvation caused by be-reavement, loneliness, apathy or illness.

• When chewing or digestive difficulties had led to a narrowing of the diet. Comments such as 'meat is difficult to chew'; 'I think eggs are binding'; 'cheese seems to give me indigestion' sometimes may stem from imaginary complaints, but in some cases there may be a genuine dislike or intolerance, so it is important to encourage alternatives and provide a wide variety of protein-rich foods.

The mean daily protein intake of all our subjects was 58 g but ranges were wide, as shown in Figures 8 and 9.

Fig. 8
AVERAGE DAILY PROTEIN INTAKE
26 males

☒ Subjects aged 65 up to 75
☐ Subjects aged 75 and over
(1 square represents 1 subject)

protein (grams)

45 - 49	
50 - 54	☒☒☐
55 - 59	☒
60 - 64	☒☒☒☐☐☐
65 - 69	☒
70 - 74	☒☐☐
75 - 79	☒
80 - 84	☒
85 - 89	☐
90 - 94	
95 - 99	
100 - 104	☐☐

Note to Figures 8 and 9

Recommended Daily Intakes (DHSS, 1969); 1979 recommendations are given in parenthesis.

Men	— 65–75 years	59 g (60 g)
	75 years and over	53 g (54 g)
Women	— 55–75 years	51 g (47 g)
	75 years and over	48 g (42 g)

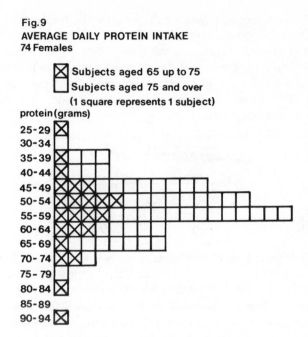

Fig. 9
AVERAGE DAILY PROTEIN INTAKE
74 Females

☒ Subjects aged 65 up to 75
☐ Subjects aged 75 and over
(1 square represents 1 subject)

The range of protein intake from the delivered meal was also wide (anything from 8 g to 58 g being consumed in one meal).

Table 8
Average Daily Protein Intake

		26 Men Protein intake (g)	74 Women Protein intake (g)
Average of whole week	mean	67	55
	range	47–103	28–90
Meals-on-wheels days	mean	67	56
	range	42–111	24–101
Delivered meal	mean	30	28
	range	19–58	8–50
Other weekdays	mean	67	54
	range	49–102	30–100
Weekends	mean	66	56
	range	42–101	23–98

The average protein intake for the whole week, meals-on-wheels days, the other weekdays and weekends — with details of the amount of protein provided by the delivered meal — are shown in Table 8. This table shows that the *mean* daily intakes of protein for men and women were above the recommendations (see Figures 8 and 9). They showed no appreciable change on days when meals-on-wheels were delivered.

The recommendations for protein are based on the fact that, in accordance with dietary habits in the UK, for most people at least 10% of their total energy intake comes from protein. In fact for the majority this figure is between 10–15% and most of our subjects were within these limits. However, some elderly individuals have very small energy intakes and in this case protein may be used for some energy purposes normally supplied by fats and carbohydrates; hence more protein would be required. With an already low protein intake, these individuals may be at risk of protein deficiency.

Nevertheless, with the type of diet consumed in the UK, which has bread as its staple food (12% energy in the form of protein), for most people the percentage of protein will almost invariably be adequate, even on an unimaginative diet.

In our survey, six subjects were consuming a diet mainly of biscuits, cakes and sometimes bread, with numerous cups of tea and cordial, and relatively large quantities of butter and sugar. Even these were barely below the 10% protein energy (9·1–9·8%). However they had survived to an advanced age (average age 83, range 70–90 years). Only two said they would like to have more meals-on-wheels delivered to them: one even failed to eat the meals provided by his daughter.

It must be realised that diets based on cereals, biscuits or bread are not necessarily deficient in protein. This is not say that such unimaginative diets should be advocated. It is stated (DHSS, 1969) 'It cannot be emphasized too highly that in the construction of diets attention must be paid to palatability as well as to nutrient content'.

Food is also for enjoyment!

It has been recommended (Exton-Smith and Stanton, 1965) that the protein content of club or domiciliary meals, that includes meals-on-wheels, should be not less than 25 g, i.e. approximately half the RDI for protein for elderly men and women (DHSS, 1969). The mean protein content of the 200 meals-on-wheels examined in our survey was 28 g, which would appear to be satisfactory. As we have seen, however, the range was wide: 8–58 g.

In fact, 73 meals (36·5%) contributed less than the recommended 25 g to the day's diet: however, in 11 of these meals some of the food provided had been left uneaten. In the meal contributing only 8 g of protein, the pudding of prunes and custard was not eaten, but even more to the point the meat portion served was very small (only 0·67 oz of roast beef) and that mainly accounted for the low protein content.

Sixteen subjects fared particularly badly because in each of their two delivered meals they consumed less than 25 g protein. For ten of these subjects plate wastage could not be blamed because they ate all the food provided.

How Much Meat?

For the majority of our subjects, meat of various types was by far the most popular food in their general diet (see page 110). How well did meals-on-wheels satisfy this choice?

Stanton (1971) suggested portion weights for meat in domiciliary meals as: 1½ oz (small), 2 oz (normal); therefore in our survey the size of the meat portions was examined. The weights of some of the most commonly served main meat dishes were as follows:

Roast meat (beef, lamb or pork) was served for 50 of the 200 investigated meals. The average portion weight of meat consumed was 1·4 oz, range 0·5–3·0 oz. In 45 of these meals, the meat portion consumed was less than 2 oz: 15 contributed 1½–2 oz; 24 contributed 1–1½ oz; 6 contributed under 1 oz (in two of these wastage had occurred).

It should be noted that in the majority of the meals (40 of the 50) where roast meat was served, the protein content of the whole meal was less than 25 g. Moreover, it should be remembered that meat is not only providing protein but is an important source of fat, minerals and vitamins, including iron and the B vitamins.

Lamb chops were served for 27 of the 200 investigated meals. The average edible portion weight was 2·7 oz., range 1·2–6·0 oz (so the size of the delivered chops varied greatly). In five of these meals the edible portion was less than 2 oz; one contributed less than 1½ oz. No wastage occurred in any of these meals, but it should be noted that in about half of the meals (14 of the 27) in which lamb chops were served, the protein content of the whole meal was less than 25 g.

Steak and kidney pie or pudding was served for 53 of the 200 investigated meals. Steak and kidney and gravy were either served with pastry as a complete pie or pudding, or with the pastry separate. In the latter case, the weight of pastry was added to our calculations to give a complete dish.

The amount of pastry served separately ranged from less than 1 oz to 3 oz. The portion of steak and kidney pie or pudding (including pastry) varied widely: although the average portion consumed was 5·9 oz, anything from less than 1½ ozs to over ½ lb meat was served (i.e. range 1·4 to 8·4 oz). But in only 6 of the 53 meals in which steak and kidney pie or pudding was served was the protein content of the whole meal less than 25 g.

The meals-on-wheels failing to meet the 25 g protein content were in the main those which contained the more expensive sources of protein, i.e. roast meat and lamb chops. So should one advise that cheaper sources of protein be substituted? Not, in my opinion, if this cheaper alternative is less popular; certainly, the roast meats and chops were among the meals most looked forward to by the recipients.

Instead, the recommendation could be that when for economy small portions of roast meats and chops are served, particular attention should be paid to the other protein components of the meal. But this recommendation may not be effective if economy goes too far. When the slice of roast meat was thinned down to 1 oz or less, the protein content of the meal fell below 25 g even when milk and cereals were added in foods such as Yorkshire pudding and milk desserts.

It may well be that with rising prices, the recipes and menus of the delivered meals will have to face changes. Textured vegetable protein might be included — but surely only if it proves acceptable and is considerably cheaper than the more familiar meat; nutritionally it does not completely replace meat. Now that fish is no longer cheaply available at the fish and chip shops, it may become important to supply fish, even though it is expensive, in more of the delivered meals-on-wheels. If fried fish is served, remember that most batters soften unpleasantly; a yeast batter is better able to withstand the long, warm holding times of meal-on-wheels deliveries.

Meals-on-wheels and luncheon club meals are subsidised and this may well prove an important factor in supplying protein foods in an attractive, familiar and varied form to old age pensioners faced with alarming rises in food prices.

Results of the social questionnaire

WERE THE AIMS OF THE PORTSMOUTH MEALS-ON-WHEELS SERVICE BEING MET?

As stated in Chapter 5, according to the Director of Social Services in Portsmouth, the aims of the meals-on-wheels service were:

1 To give the nutritional benefit of at least two meals per week to those completely housebound.
2 To satisfy a temporary need, e.g. return from hospital or incapacity due to injury.
3 To give regular social contact, help to identify deterioration, and introduce other welfare services.

The reason the 100 subjects in our survey were receiving meals-on-wheels was examined under two separate headings, (a) the original reason, given in the records (question 10) and (b) the present reason, in the opinion of the subject (question 11).

Reason for receipt of meals-on-wheels	Original reason (data from the Portsmouth records) Number of subjects	Present reason (opinion of subjects) Number of subjects
Housebound	10	32
Bedridden	0	1
Return from hospital	16	0
Injury	5	5
Illness	20	15
Recent bereavement	3	0
Living alone	10	39
Unknown (no records)	36	8

The length of time that meals-on-wheels had been received was also checked from the Portsmouth records and from the question put to the subject.

As can be seen below, the subject was not always accurate, but in most of the cases where the records did not provide the answer, the subjects thought they had received them for a long time (two years or more).

Receipt of Meals-on-Wheels

Length of time	(Question 8) Answer from Portsmouth records	(Question 7) Answer from subject
less than 1 month	2	1
1 month–5 months	1	4
6 months–11 months	8	14
1 year–1 year 11 months	24	20
2 years and more	46	61
unknown	19	0

It would seem that, although recipients were generally placed on the meals-on-wheels list according to the aims of the Portsmouth meals-on-wheels service, there was at the time of this survey a need for a review of the list. Such a review might reveal the reasons for continuing delivery of meals to those classified as reason 'unknown'. (Note: second column is opinion of recipient.) It might also have led to an explanation of why the majority of subjects had been placed on the list over two years previously and why so few additions had been made during the last six months.

SOCIAL AND WELFARE CONTACTS THROUGH MEALS-ON-WHEELS

The aim 'to give regular social contact, help to identify deterioration, and introduce other welfare services' was investigated by questions number 39, 40, 42 and 46 in the social questionnaire (see Appendix B).

Thirty six per cent of the subjects said they never had visits from local authority officers, 2% were receiving daily visits and 29% were receiving visits every 3 months.

Voluntary help came mostly from the people delivering meals-on-wheels, thus achieving the aims of 3 above (page 107); 84% said they never had a visit from any other voluntary workers (although as will be seen later, many were well visited by friends, neighbours or relatives).

It is not known whether the subjects paid visits to or received visits from doctors or medical auxiliaries on the advice of meals-on-wheels workers who might have observed health deterioration. Forty-seven per cent said they never had a visit from a doctor or medical auxiliary. However, a weekly or monthly visit was received by 35%. As 77% of our subjects were of limited mobility it is not surprising that 70% did not get out to pay a visit to a doctor or medical auxiliary. However 25% paid either monthly or three monthly visits.

OTHER QUESTIONS FROM THE SOCIAL QUESTIONNAIRE

In order to assess the people with whom we are dealing, the investigator's subjective assessment of subject's competence (which was stated at the end of the questionnaire) is given below:

Competence (Questions 71–73)

Mental	Fully Alert 69%	Adequate 29%	Confused 2%
Physical	Fully Mobile & Competent 23%	Limited Mobility 76%	Helpless 1%
Over-all dependency	Independent 22%	Partially Dependent 63%	Wholly Dependent 15%

Although answers to all the questions in the social questionnaire (Appendix B) were available for analysis, several of the questions are not further referred to in this book because it was felt that they had little relevance to the main results obtained from Portsmouth, e.g. this was not an industrial district where redundancy or retirement played an important role, therefore the questions on date of retirement of subject or spouse are not further pursued. Should Local Authorities wish to use our questionnaires they may decide to omit some of the questions, or to ask all of them and assess their relevance at a later stage.

Marital Status (Question 27)

The majority of the subjects (68%) were widowed (included in this category were a few who were divorced or separated). Of these, 36% had been widowed or separated for 10 years or more, and one was recently bereaved. Bachelors and spinsters represented 20% of the sample. Married subjects constituted 12% of the sample (spouse not included in survey).

Household Composition (Question 35)

As would be expected from the large number of widowed or single subjects, 78% were living alone; 9% were living with relatives.

Children Living Within Five Miles (Question 28)

From Portsmouth, a distance of five miles was considered to be a reasonable distance for visiting. In other areas a shorter or longer distance might be considered reasonable, according to traffic conditions. Thirty nine per cent of our subjects had children living within five miles. 'The handicap of living alone loses its force when relatives live nearby'. (Townsend, 1963).

Favourite Foods in General Diet (Uncoded Question)

The subjects were asked if, in their general diet, they had any favourite foods. Twelve said that 'everything' was their favourite food and 24 said that they had no preferences.

The rest (64) gave their favourite foods as listed below:

Foods mentioned by name included:	No. of times mentioned
Meat of various types, including offal	58
Poultry and game	11
Fish	11
Fruit in various forms	10
Steak and kidney pie/pudding	8
Chips	7
Fruit pies/tarts	6
Eggs	5
Custards	4
Yorkshire pudding	3
Cheese, gravy, soups, tinned milk puddings	2

Seven gave answers covering many foods, e.g. cooked dinners, fresh garden produce, all home-made and natural foods, savoury things, anything tasty, savoury flavours, oven-ready dinners for one. *Other foods mentioned once were*: grape juice, Ribena, Cornish pasties, macaroni cheese, spaghetti, tinned milk, treacle pudding, sponge pudding, suet pudding, bread and butter, Birds Eye Mousse, ice-cream, chocolates, iced cakes and almond slices.

Reasons for Avoidance of Certain Foods (Uncoded Question)
Cheese: considered indigestible and 'binding' (mentioned four times). One subject could not take it because of her medication of Nardil tablets and two were purely dislikes.

Fruit: other than disliking or 'not being partial to' fruit, rhubarb was considered too acid and other subjects had chewing difficulties with fruit or considered it to be indigestible, or that it would 'bring on the pains'.

Vegetables: green vegetables were considered, by all those who gave a reason for avoidance, to be indigestible or 'binding'. There was one exception, the subject who said she could not consume green vegetables because of her medication with Nardil tablets. (She may have been confused by the usual warning to avoid broad beans with MAO inhibitors — anti-depressants.) Reasons for the avoidance of other vegetables were because they disagreed with the subject, caused indigestion or were simply disliked.

Fatty foods 'in excess' were avoided by one subject with heart trouble.

Reactions to Amounts of Different Types of Food Supplied in Meals-on-Wheels (Questions 16–22A)
As a check on reaction to the delivered meals, answers were noted to the questions in the meals-on-wheels (pink) questionnaire relating to portion size. In general, recipients indicated that the servings were of acceptable size. However, four points are worth noting:

1 30% of recipients would have liked a larger portion of meat.
2 46% found that the servings of potatoes were too large.
3 24% would have liked a larger portion of a second vegetable (potatoes were 'first vegetable').
4 24% said there was too little gravy, 17% said there was too little custard.

Type of Main Dish and Dessert Most Enjoyed in Meals-on-Wheels.
When asked to classify the types of main dishes and desserts most enjoyed in the delivered meals, the answers were as follows:

Main Dish: no preference expressed (36%); most popular main dish was roast dinner (39%). Others in order of preference were pies and puddings (13%), stews (9%), fish (3%).

Dessert: no preference expressed (33%); most popular dessert was sponge type pudding (28%). Others in order of preference were pastry/tarts (16%), stewed fruit (15%), milk pudding (8%).

Would You Like To Have Meals-on-Wheels More Often Than you Do? (Question 12)
One question in the meals-on-wheels questionnaire which the recipients were asked was hypothetical: 'Would you like to have meals-on-wheels more often that you do, if YES, on how many days per week?' It was explained to them that there was little likelihood of any increase in the immediate future in the number of delivered meals, since there were no facilities at present, but that we would like to know their wishes.

It should be observed that the answer to this question could only be subjective. It could be that, given a hypothetical question, the subjects were content to keep the status quo. On the contrary it could be argued that, because they were in effect being offered a 'pipe dream' they might ask for more than they really wanted. This question could only explore the wishes of the recipients.

Factors Which Might Influence Requests For More Delivered Meals
There could be a number of reasons why the recipients may or may not ask for more meals-on-wheels (m/w). Two-way computer tabulations showed whether the following had any significance:

Opinion of the meal (Table xi, page 191) — Question 13.
Length of time m/w had been supplied (Table xii, page 192) — Question 7.
Ability to cook own meal (Table xiii, page 193) — Question 63.
Mobility (Table xiv, page 193) — Question 72
Composition of household (Table xv, page 194) — Question 35.
Visits from relatives (Table xvi, page 195) — Question 37.
Visits from friends and neighbours (Table xvii page 196) — Question 38.

There were three additional factors which may have influenced their answers:

- They might have been too proud to ask for more help. (This was investigated by studying the case histories.)
- They might feel the cost of more than two m/w per week would be prohibitive. (This was checked against the individual's estimated weekly budget for food.)
- They may have preferred to eat out rather than to have meals brought in. (We investigated how many times the subject had eaten out.)

It should be noted that 94% of the people in this survey classed the meals as excellent (22%), good (44%) or adequate (28%). Praise could not be too high for all the helpers in the Portsmouth m/w service. However, when asked whether they would like to receive more m/w per week (Question 12) the answers were as follows:

content with 2 m/w per week — 59%
content with 3 m/w per week — 21%
content with 4 m/w per week — 9%
content with 5 m/w per week — 4%
content with 6 m/w per week — 0%
content with 7 m/w per week — 7%

Opinion of the Meal
Fifty-six people who classed the meals as excellent, good or adequate were among the 59 who did *not* want more than 2 per week. This is shown in Table xi, p. 191.

Clearly it was not dislike of the food that caused the recipients to decline the possibility of additional meals. Five subjects thought the meal 'poor', yet two of these wanted them delivered daily!

Length of Time Meals-on-Wheels had been supplied
Of the 7 who wanted daily delivery, 6 had received m/w for more than a year (Table xii page 192). Boredom did not seem to be the reason for the refusal of the possibility of daily m/w.

Ability to Prepare own Meal
Table xiii (page 193) shows that 19 subjects needed other people to prepare the main meal for them on the days when m/w were not delivered. Of these, 11 were quite happy with the twice weekly delivery, another 6 would have liked 3 deliveries a week. It would seem that even if they were not able to prepare their own meal the

majority were content to have other people preparing the main meal for them. Preparing meals for themselves did not seem to be too much trouble for 48 out of the 59 who were content with the present twice weekly delivery.

Mobility

Only one was bedridden and therefore put into the category of 'helpless' but she was content with the twice weekly delivery. Of the 76 who were considered to be of limited mobility, 46 were also happy with the present arrangement but it may be significant that of the 7 who would have liked a daily delivery, 6 were of limited mobility (Table xiv, page 193).

Composition of Household

Those who live alone often lose the incentive to prepare meals for themselves but of the 78 subjects living alone, 63 were happy with either 2 or 3 meals-on-wheels per week. Again it may be significant that of the 7 who wanted the daily delivery, 6 were living alone (Table xv, page 194).

Visits from Friends, Neighbours and Relatives

In Portsmouth there was already strong support for our 100 elderly subjects from relatives, friends and neighbours, who often helped with shopping, provision of meals or gifts of food.

Table xvi (page 195) shows that 12 subjects never had visits from relatives and Table xvii (page 196) shows that 16 never had visits from friends and neighbours. Some of these subjects may have come into both categories, i.e. never had visits from friends, neighbours or relatives. However only one or two of these socially isolated people asked for a daily contact with the lady delivering m/w.

Pride

Two admitted that pride prevented them from asking for more deliveries. One man did not see why he should be 'taking money out of the ratepayers' pockets', while one woman did not like her neighbours to know that she was receiving meals-on-wheels. Both were glad to be receiving the present twice weekly deliveries.

Possible Prohibitive Cost of the Meal

When the cost of the delivered meal was raised from 2s 0d to 2s 6d in May 1970 only 6 out of a total of 325 receiving meals-on-wheels decided not to continue. Only 3 mentioned cost as a reason for not asking for more meals-on-wheels, although one of these spent more on fish and chips — which his wife liked — than he would have spent on extra m/w. There was no relation between the weekly estimated amount spent on food and the number of extra meals wanted.

Eating Out

Of the 59 who did not want extra meals delivered, 43 never ate meals with friends, 55 never ate in restaurants and 46 never ate out at luncheon clubs. It was not because they were already eating out that they refused the possibility of extra delivered meals. However, in spite of the fact that in Portsmouth meals-on-wheels were at that period meant to be restricted to people not able to attend luncheon clubs, in practice 19 subjects ate at a luncheon club once a week, 3 twice a week and 2 three times a week, and these luncheon club meals were preferred to extra meals-on-wheels.

Age and Sex of Recipient

There was no evidence that more meals-on-wheels were required by the older recipients but a higher proportion of the men asked for more delivered meals a week.

Injury

Determination to manage in spite of infirmities was apparent. Of the 5 people incapacitated through injury, 4 expressed satisfaction with 2 meals-on-wheels per week.

Shopping (Question 64)

With 77% of limited mobility and 78% either partially or wholly dependent on others, it is not surprising that 66% had others (generally home helps) to do their shopping for them. A subjective assessment was made of shopping lists to see whether there was an appreciable difference in the types of food bought when these elderly men and women were unable to shop for themselves. There appeared to be little difference whether or not they did their own shopping, although one woman who could not get to the shops made the point that she wished she could get out to see for herself what was available for variety; several referred to the inconvenience and weight of large packs. The importance of home helps or others for shopping is apparent. Occasional reliable help to get to the shops may be even more appreciated than shopping always brought in.

Cost of Foodstuffs (Question 65)

When asked to estimate the money spent on food for home consumption (i.e. food ingredients or meals, excluding meals-on-wheels, bought to eat at home), the majority were found to be vague and *not too much reliance could be placed on their answers*, which were *estimates* of weekly expenditure (in 1970, it must be remembered) on food for home consumption by subject only (i.e. not including spouse or any other person):

up to 19s 11d	...	1
£1 — £1 9s 11d	...	18
£1 10s — £1 19s 11d	...	44
£2 0s 0d — £2 9s 11d	...	27
£2 10s — £2 19s 11d	...	8
£3 and over	...	2

Note: the retirement pension in 1970 was £5 0s 0d.

Pets (Question 66)

Old age pensioners are frequently depicted as being dependent for company on their pets, particularly budgerigars, cats or dogs. In answer to the question 'Do you keep any pets and how much is spent weekly on their food?' (including domestic animals and wild birds), these were the numbers of subjects answering within the groups given:

Answers	No. of Subjects
No pets	77
up to 11d	6
1s 0d — 1s 11d	3
2s 0d — 4s 11d	6
5s 0d — 9s 11d	6
10s 0d and over	2

One pensioner spent between 25s 0d and 30s 0d weekly on food for her old cat, which was very fat. On herself she spent between 30s and £2 which included 10s 0d per week for five midday meals provided by a neighbour; she had money left over to spend on religious books.

Special Diets (Questions 67–68A)

In answer to the question 'Are you on a special diet?', 9 said they were. Of these, 4 were self-imposed diets and 5 were recommended by a doctor.

Of the self-imposed diets, 2 subjects had been on low fat diets for more than ten years; one other had been diagnosed as a diabetic in 1942 and said she had put herself on a diet. The fourth subject had also been on a diet for more than ten years, avoiding 'strong greens', gravy, custard, sauces, rice pudding, eggs, cheese and liver; the reason given was that all these were constipating.

Of the five diets recommended by a doctor, three were diabetic (two diagnosed seven years, one over twenty years ago); one was a gastric diet and the fifth excluded cheese, Bovril, Oxo, Marmite, broad beans and alcohol (presumably because these are excluded when taking certain antidepressants).

There was, however, one who said he was not on a special diet but whose comments in the case history are worth recording:

Subject 32 (a man in his early eighties) had been ordered a 'low calorie' diet by his doctor, but gave one look at the diet sheet and as he felt everything he liked or found easy to prepare was forbidden, he tore it up saying that at his time of life he was not going to give up eating pleasures just to live a few weeks longer. Incidentally, this gentleman was one of the few surviving participants in our follow-up survey (see Chapter 11) ten years later!

Time Limit of Last Drink (Question 68B)

The importance of fluid as well as food is well recognised. Does fear of incontinence lead some elderly people to limit fluid intake, with the possible risk of dehydration? Of the 19 who said that they did limit the time of fluid intake, none mentioned incontinence. Seven said they tried to avoid rising at night but the principal reasons given were hip injury or arthritis.

Medication (Question 69)

All but 17 were taking some form of medication (including health foods). The classifications are given below:

Answers to 'Do you take any of the following?'

aperient	... 6
tablets and medicines	... 44
health foods	... 2
aperient and tablets and medicines	... 20
aperient and health foods	... 0
tablets (or medicine) and health foods	... 9
aperient and tablets (or medicine) and health foods	... 2
none	... 17

Refrigeration (Uncoded question)

Seventyeight per cent of subjects did not possess a refrigerator. One with a refrigerator only stored butter in it and kept it disconnected because he believed electricity to be dangerous.

Investigators drew attention in case histories to unhygienic washing up and poor storage facilities; some subjects were observed storing mouldy bread, and milk puddings 'on the turn'. It was felt that a number were running a risk of food poisoning. This was accentuated by the fact that elderly people are advised to keep their rooms warm to cut down risk of hypothermia; but frequently their warm room is also used as their larder. So food was not only unrefrigerated, it was also being stored under warm conditions.

Cooking Facilities (Uncoded question)
All had cooking facilities, although one used a paraffin heater; 88% used a gas cooker or ring, 11% used electricity.

SOCIAL CIRCUMSTANCES AS THEY AFFECT WEIGHT CHANGES

Approximately twelve months after the recorded and weighed diet survey one of our investigators returned to the subjects to assess whether their meal pattern, health, circumstances or mobility had changed. The meal pattern was assessed from a food recall of a day's diet. The investigator compared this with the food recall (see Appendix B) of the previous year and cross-checked with the previous year's detailed diet record. The majority, according to the investigator, were not only eating the same amounts of the same foods but were even sitting in the same position in the same chair. However, a number of changes in meal pattern, health, circumstances and mobility were noted.

The circumstances of the 11 who showed a change of weight of 4 kg or more were examined in detail. Five of them had been classified as depressed. All of these had lost weight except one who had gained 9·6 kg. *Subject No. 38* (classified as depressed) found providing meals for himself to be a great effort; he even found reheating meals-on-wheels a nuisance. A neighbour who used to help with food had died. *Subject No. 54* (classified as depressed) had moved to a corporation flat and was no longer receiving meals or help with shopping from neighbours. *Subject No. 42*, who had not been classified as depressed, had in fact been bereaved by the death of his wife. *Subject No. 21* had lost a neighbour who had moved out of the district. This neighbour had previously provided many meals; another neighbour could only supply Sunday lunch.

Illness probably contributed to the loss of weight of three subjects and a reducing diet to the loss of weight of a fourth.

Recommendations which stem from some of these sociological findings are made in the final chapter.

In addition, we collaborated with two separate studies on volunteers from our original sample of 100 men and women.

Seventy-five participated in a pilot survey relating dietary selection to dental state (Heath 1972). The range of specific common foods included in their diet was found to be partially related to the dentures used, or not used, for chewing. Despite wide variations, the dental state of these pensioners was, in general, poor. Eighty-eight per cent were without natural teeth (edentulous), and of these 24% used only their upper or nether dentures for chewing, and 68% had dentures graded 'poor' or 'very poor'. Only 36% of these edentulous men and women thought they needed any dental treatment, and only two had sought treatment.

Seventy-two participated in a pilot winter study of body temperatures related to their environmental temperatures and living conditions (Fox *et al.* 1973). No case of serious hypothermia was found, but the investigation confirmed that elderly people have lower body temperatures, and suggested that the coldest individuals tended to be least aware of discomfort from the cold; this may well place them 'at risk' for developing hypothermia.

10
Assessment of nutritional risk in individual subjects

Local Authorities may be faced with the alternative of providing a 5–7 day a week meals-on-wheels service to a restricted number of people (putting others on a waiting list) or providing a more limited service (say one or two meals per week) to a greater number of recipients and thereby possibly cutting down on, or eliminating, the waiting list.

This chapter reviews the situation in Portsmouth where two meals-on-wheels per week were delivered to 325 people over the age of 65, and looks for simple ways of ascertaining which, if any, of the recipients needed more. We later look at possible simple ways of assessing urgency of need for those not yet receiving delivered meals; and for re-assessment, as the client's circumstances may alter.

It is realised that most Local Authorities wishing to investigate the adequacy of their meals-on-wheels service are unable to afford the time or money to conduct a week's weighed dietary survey with computer analysis. The data were, therefore, studied for possible short cuts — not requiring the detailed weighing or the computer — which might help to point to individual subjects at special nutritional risk.

There is no absolute criterion of malnutrition. It is stressed in the previous chapters that Recommended Daily Amounts are recommendations for groups of the population and that individual requirements are not known. Therefore even information collected from detailed weighing of food and analysed intake is insufficient *for the individual*. Because there is a need to identify individuals who may be at special nutritional risk, this chapter investigates possible indices of 'at risk' factors.

One possible test is to look at social data. A visiting social worker, or other trained interviewer, could gather the type of information collected in case studies by our investigators. The social data from our survey were compared with our information from the full calculated nutrient intakes. As an alternative short cut to using the nutrient intake, the social data were also compared with information from the meal pattern (shopping list and 24 hour diet recall); and with information from the weighed diet record. Throughout this investigation of possible 'at risk' factors the number of main meals consumed by each subject was considered, together with other indices.

If short cuts could be found from our data, it might be possible for a Local Authority briefly to investigate recipients, or would-be recipients, of meals-on-wheels and thus find the individuals in the area who might be in need of extra help.

It is recognised that malnutrition among the elderly is generally multifactorial. It would therefore be surprising if only one short cut index could be used to point to all those in need of extra help. Several possible short cuts were therefore considered. Each was examined in turn (after a detailed study of all 100 files) to see which group of short cut indices would together be most likely to pick out all the subjects who might be at nutritional risk.

1 Shopping List and Recall

Evidence was considered from the estimated weekly shopping list, and the 24 hour diet recall. Both of these are contained in the blue paper uncoded questionnaire (Appendix B), and were obtained from only brief questioning in one interview.

2 Dietary Record

Evidence was considered from the seven-day record of food items consumed.

Frequency of Consumption of Food Items

Marr et al. (1961) suggested that a count of the number of times in the week each type of food was consumed could give a picture of nutrient intake, without the necessity of weighing. Their method used a factor based on the weight of an average helping of each type of food. Amounts consumed by our elderly subjects showed a wide range, so that an average weight factor might be misleading. Further work by Marr (personal communication) showed that — even though their sample was limited to bank clerks with a fairly regular pattern of eating — no accurate picture of nutrient intake could be obtained from this method.

'Protein Meals'

Exton-Smith and Stanton (1965) found some correlation between the state of health, as assessed in 44 subjects, and the number of main meals eaten. They suggested that further work would be useful to discover whether the number of main meals and the amount of milk consumed would give a rough assessment of the consumption of protein. They suggested that it is among subjects unable to supply data for a week's weighed survey that the danger of malnutrition is most likely.

Stanton (1971) divided subjects into categories according to total number of protein meals eaten weekly (a protein meal is defined as one containing not less than 1 oz of meat, 2 oz of fish, 1 oz of cheese or one egg). This is a very small amount of protein, and is therefore probably more significant in highlighting consumption of a main meal or snack than in showing a high intake of protein. Obviously it is simple to identify a protein meal; only a limited amount of weighing, if any, is necessary.

Stanton's poorest category was 8 or less protein meals weekly

The next category was 9–13 protein meals weekly

The top group was 14 or more protein meals weekly.

It was decided to consider this 'protein meals' pattern, plus other indices.

3 Milk

Milk intake of our subjects was noted. Stanton (1971) had found that most of her top category subjects (consuming 14 or more protein meals weekly) were also consuming 7 or more pints of milk a week.

4 Vitamin C

Because Stanton had recorded, with the meals pattern, the amount of citrus fruit, tomatoes or green vegetables eaten, our calculated data on individual vitamin C intakes was noted. Largely due to delays between cooking and consumption (see Chapter 8) true (analysed) vitamin C intakes on days when meals-on-wheels were delivered were generally lower than the values which might be expected from Food Tables calculations. A calculated average of 0–29 mg vitamin C per day was therefore classed as 'poor intake' even though a calculated value nearing 29 mg might normally be classed as adequate.

5 Other Indices

Finally, the data were studied for other possible indices of nutritional risk:

- Wastage from meals-on-wheels.
- An apathetic approach to eating after the main lunch time meal.
- Subjective evidence of depression.
- Inability to get to the shops for food.
- Marked changes in weight.
- Receipt of supplementary benefit.
- Weekly intakes. To estimate whether the computer print-out would add essential information which would otherwise be missed, the following weekly intakes of each subject were noted as possible indicators of the quality of the diet: total protein, iron, potassium, potassium/1000 kcal, carbohydrate and carbohydrate/energy %.
- Individual case studies. These were fully examined.

RESULTS AND DISCUSSION

Shopping List and 24 hour Diet Recall

Evaluation of shopping list and 24 hour diet recall showed that in most cases these gave a fairly good picture of the diet as compared with the weighed diet record. However, in some cases the lists and recalls gave a distorted picture of food intake.

Subject 12: Her shopping list indicated a pint of milk daily. In fact, most of the bread, butter and milk purchased was allowed to get stale and was thrown away. Furthermore, diet recall optimistically indicated a roast chicken midday meal as typical of the type of meal pattern followed. This would have been an indication of a good meal pattern, but in the case history it was recorded that she said she was not interested in food. Nothing had been taken from the store-cupboard during the week. A neighbour brought her a midday cup of tea but the social contact was more important to her than the drink, which she usually left to get cold. She wasted half the roast beef and roast potatoes and the whole portion of rice pudding in one of her delivered meals. Consequently neither shopping list nor recall was correct.

Subject 13: The diet recall indicated three protein meals a day as her normal pattern, but weighed diet record showed only 8 protein meals in the week.

Subject 27: The diet recall showed a cooked breakfast of bacon and fried bread. In the week's diet record this was only recorded twice, at other times she had uncooked breakfasts, e.g. cereals or biscuits. On the contrary the shopping list was more gloomy than the actual intake. It stated that although fish was liked she could not obtain it locally. Diet record showed 6 oz fish at one meal, and at another meal a portion of canned salmon (not itemised under 'purchases of canned goods').

Subject 50: It needed the week's weighed diet record to show that this lady was a very erratic eater. Her shopping list was over optimistic, e.g. 1 lb tomatoes, 6 eggs. She actually ate ¼ lb tomatoes and 2 eggs. The investigator noted that some of the food bought was never eaten, it was either thrown away or given to her old cat.

Total reliance on brief evidence from shopping lists and 24 hour diet recall has a further disadvantage: until confidence can be gained during the course of a week, investigation of larder stocks is often resented. Even a week's recorded diet was found to be misleading in a study of elderly women living alone unless use of food from larder stocks was taken into account (Platt *et al*, 1964). The rapport built up by our investigators generally made it easy for them to see the use made of larder stocks, or to note the absence of an emergency food store.

Division of our Subjects into 'Protein Meal' Categories
27% of sample: — 8 or fewer 'meals' per week
45% of sample: — 9–13 'meals' per week
28% of sample: — 14 or more 'meals' per week

Lowest Category (8 or fewer 'meals' per week)
In Stanton's survey, between 5 and 7 of the meals consumed by her lowest category subjects were supplied by meals-on-wheels or clubs. Our 27 lowest category subjects were receiving only two delivered meals; the rest of the meals came from their own efforts, or from neighbours, relatives or friends, and occasionally one or two meals from clubs. Of our lowest category subjects, 22 were managing to have 7 or 8 'protein meals' per week. Two consumed only 6 and three consumed only 5. From the case histories it was obvious that at least nine of the 27 lowest category subjects needed extra help to improve their diets. On more detailed reappraisal, a further eight would be recommended for extra help in addition to their present two meals-on-wheels.

Middle Category (9–13 'meals' per week)
The majority of the 45 in the middle category of 9–13 'meals'

showed little sign from the case studies of being at risk. There were exceptions, and 11 would probably have been helped by extra meals-on-wheels or nutritional advice, for example:

> *Subject 59:* Ate 11 'meals', but relied on receiving the two meals-on-wheels and a club meal. On three days she had virtually nothing to eat after lunch.

> *Subject 65:* Ate 10 'meals' during the survey week, ½ pint milk daily, but on three days had virtually nothing to eat after lunch. Very apathetic towards the preparation of food.

> *Subject 85:* On the week of the survey had 11 'meals' and 1 pint milk daily, but she is normally apathetic towards food and sometimes the two meals-on-wheels are her only cooked meals of the week.

Top Category (14 or more 'meals' per week)

Even in the top category of 14 or more 'meals' weekly there was obviously need for a case study and observation throughout the week, as well as for a counting of 'meals'. Three top category subjects would probably have benefited from extra meals-on-wheels, for example:

> *Subject 80:* Her diet record showed 15 'meals' during the survey week and ½ pint milk daily. However the investigator reported 'she sits for many hours at a stretch, going without food, and says she can only eat when the mood takes her'. The reason given in the records for her receiving meals-on-wheels was 'she neglects herself'. She obviously had no regular meal pattern; the 15 meals of the survey week were not an indication of a top category subject, since the investigator's report suggested that this might not be a regular pattern.

Table xviii (Appendix A, page 197), shows the calculated nutrient intakes of subjects in the lowest category compared with subjects in the top category. As an example, two groups of the same sex and age are compared, i.e. females aged 65–74 years. It can be seen that in general with regard to group nutrient intakes the 'meals' criterion does not markedly distinguish between the lowest group of subjects and the top group. Moreover, the case studies quoted above of some of those in the middle and top categories have shown that the 'meals' criterion is not infallible.

As far as individuals are concerned Table xviii also confirms that nutrient intakes can be misleading. *Subjects 68, 69 and 86* had a protein intake above 50 g, yet were in the bottom meals category.

Milk Consumption

Stanton (1971) found that most of her top category subjects had a milk consumption of 7 or more pints per week. In our survey (see Table xix, Appendix A, page 198) the daily milk consumption of the top category subjects was similar to that of the poorest category.

	Top category subjects	Lowest category subjects
1 pint or over	6	5
½–¾ pint	15	13
under ½ pint	7	9

There was no evidence of a relationship between meal pattern and milk consumption.

Vitamin C Intake

In evaluating adequacy of diet, Stanton (1971) used as an index the amount of citrus fruit, green vegetables or tomatoes eaten, whereas in our survey we calculated vitamin C intake by using Food Tables.

Table xix shows that 4 of the lowest category subjects had high vitamin C intakes (one of them averaged 113 mg per day by taking Ribena on cereals). In all three meals categories there were low vitamin C intakes. There was no evidence of a relationship between meal pattern and vitamin C intake.

However, a combination of few protein 'meals', low milk intake and low vitamin C intake may well be indicative of a generally poor diet. Of the four who had this combination, subjects 12, 15 and 20 had been noted in the case histories as being in need of extra help; and subject 22 had lost 6·3 kg in weight when re-weighed a year later. It was therefore decided to keep a 'score' on all subjects, noting other possible signs of an 'at risk' situation. The resultant score sheet is given in Table xx (Appendix A, pp. 200–6). A mark has been placed in the appropriate column for each subject where a possible 'at risk' factor was observed, i.e. poorest category meals; under ½ pint milk daily; only 0–29 mg vitamin C daily; wastage in meals-on-wheels, etc.

Wastage from Meals-on-Wheels

Food wastage from a delivered meal may be an indication that enough has been eaten, of an unpopular meal, or over-large servings, and may point to a need for an improved menu and/or cooking practices. However, in our survey the delivered meals were generally popular and seemed, apart from over-generous helpings of potato, to provide servings of acceptable size. There was no statistical evidence of a relationship between meal pattern and meals-on-wheels wastage. However, the high proportion of poor category subjects who left not only potato, but meat and other parts of the delivered meal uneaten (see Table xix, page 198) indicates that food wastage from a meal that has been provided could be regarded as a possible 'at risk' factor.

Nothing after Lunchtime

Those who had nothing more to eat after lunch except a beverage and biscuit, cake or plain bread and butter were classified as consuming 'nothing' as it was felt to signify apathy towards food. If this happened only once during the week it was not considered to be significant and is not noted in Table xix, page 198). One subject in the top category who never ate anything after lunch was doing so on doctor's orders after a very good breakfast and lunch and was also not included in the table.

The majority ate breakfast (mostly uncooked, e.g. cereals and/or toast and marmalade; some cooked, e.g. egg, bacon); this was generally followed by a mid-morning beverage (sometimes with biscuit); the majority ate a two-course lunch (only two ate their main meal in the evening); the period at which least food was taken was generally at tea (e.g. beverage, sandwich, cake) and at high tea/supper time; but most subjects ate easy snacks, e.g. a portion of cheese or ham or a tomato.

The number of times 'nothing' was eaten after lunch was:

Top category	Middle category	Lowest category
Nil	1 subject 5 times	4 subjects 7 times
	6 subjects 3 times	1 subject 6 times
	5 subjects twice	1 subject 5 times
		3 subjects 3 times
		2 subjects twice

There was no evidence to *discount* a relationship between few protein meals and 'nothing' eaten after lunch ($\chi^2 = 10.25$ p <0.01). It would therefore seem advisable to include this type of meal pattern as a risk factor pointing to the need for further investigation and possible help.

> *Subject 15:* enjoyed meals-on-wheels because they added variety to her rather monotonous diet. She was looked after socially: a neighbour brought a cup of tea to her in bed in the morning; a day seldom passed without a visit from one member of the family and they often brought her a pie or a pudding, so she managed to eat one 'protein meal' a day. However on six occasions she ate 'nothing' after lunch. In cases such as this there would seem to be a need for a

store-cupboard stocked with easy to prepare nourishing deli-
catessen or convenience foods so that she could eat 'a little
something' with the minimum of effort.

Depression

Although there were subjects subjectively assessed as depressed in
all three 'meals' categories, the case histories show that depression
can have a severe effect on food intake:

> *Subject 98:* aged 83, admitted that she had deteriorated since
> her sister died six months ago, even though she had faced the
> strain of caring for the sister who was 'senile and incontinent'.
> She bought more milk than she needed, to have ready for
> callers. She would take even more if it would bring her
> company. She said she does not want to eat more and did not
> have incentive since her sister's death.

Because 13 of the 28 subjects in the top category meal pattern
were classed as depressed (see Table xix, page 198), their files were
studied to see whether their depression had led to compulsive eating
and obesity. But this did not seem to be the case. Only one of these
subjects, height 158 cm, weight 65·8 kg, had an eating pattern
described as 'erratic and disorganised'.

Although there was no evidence of a relationship between few
protein meals and depression, whatever the meal pattern, assessment of depression should always be considered as a possible risk
factor taken in conjunction with the other short cut indices.

Inability to Go Out Shopping

Only 4 of the 27 poorest meals category subjects were mobile
enough to shop for themselves (see Table xix, page 198). More than
half the top category subjects also needed others to shop for them.

A rough comparison of food purchases made by 'self' and 'others'
showed that there was little to choose between them. It may even be
that a home help, relative or friend can bring in more and better
food than would be purchased by the subject left to her own
devices. Only if 'others' shopping is badly done need this be
considered a risk factor.

However, enquiries to the Gerontology Nutrition Unit for
shopping advice seems to indicate that the elderly and their helpers
are aware of shopping problems and that Local Authorities, food
manufacturers and retailers should investigate means of helping the
elderly to find and use nourishing foods, including nourishing
convenience foods. 'Shopping for Food' was one of the reports of

Age Concern (1973) which drew attention to the shopping difficulties of the elderly.

The case history below illustrates the possible results of not getting to the shops:

> *Subject 6:* wanted to know if her diet could be improved, and suggestions were made for main meals on the days when she only had soup. She had never heard of many of the items suggested because she never visited the shops. She said she would be pleased to receive news of easy canned and frozen meals (including price) so that these could sometimes be added to her shopping list. A quick look in cupboards revealed no stores beyond the current weekly items such as bread, butter, biscuits, cornflakes and soup.

Weight Changes

Of the 27 people in the poorest meals category, 15 were available for re-weighing approximately one year later. Twelve had lost weight (three subjects had lost as much as 8 kg, 6·3 kg and 9·6 kg respectively). The three who had gained weight had only gained 1·4 kg, 1·4 kg and 1·9 kg respectively.

Of the 28 in the top meals category, 11 were available for re-weighing approximately one year later. Seven had gained weight (one 3·3 kg, the others between 0·6 and 1·9 kg). Four had lost weight (three only between 0·6–1·9 kg; one noted as depressed, diabetic and sleeping badly because of pains from arthritis had lost 12·6 kg).

No conclusion on the significance of weight changes can be drawn because so many subjects were not available for re-weighing through illness, death or moves from the district. However, our figures are sufficient to indicate that, when possible, weight records should be kept and weight changes should be regarded as a possible 'at risk' factor needing thorough investigation by social workers as well as doctors.

Supplementary Benefit

There was no evidence of a relationship between meal pattern and the receipt of supplementary benefit.

There would have been cause for concern had those receiving supplementary benefit not managed to achieve a meal pattern comparable to those not on supplementary benefit, because the extra money should relieve poverty sufficiently to allow for adequate purchase of food.

It should be noted that since our survey food prices have risen very considerably and this risk factor should be kept under constant review to see whether the increases in pension and supplementary benefit continue to keep step with the rises in food prices.

Nutritional Data

From Table xix there was no relationship between meal pattern and potassium intake or total carbohydrate intake.

But there is no evidence to reject the hypothesis that there is a connection between low meal pattern and low iron intake, in statistical terms ($\chi^2 = 6.18$ p <0.02), low meal pattern and high carbohydrate/energy % ($\chi^2 = 17.7$ p < 0.001) and low meal pattern and total protein intake ($\chi^2 = 9.94$ p < 0.05).

Case Studies

The case studies were examined *without reference to any other data* to see whether the information in them would be sufficient to pick out subjects at nutritional risk. It was interesting after this 'blind' assessment to refer to the marks in the score sheet (Table xx, Appendix A, pp. 200–6) and to find that in general the case study had found subjects with several 'at risk' marks.

Results

From the case studies alone it was considered that extra meals-on-wheels or luncheon club visits would probably benefit the following:

> *Subject 14:* has Paget's disease and moves with difficulty, relies on convenience foods.

> *Subject 16:* avoids cooking in kitchen because she says any noise disturbs the neighbours, who then bang on the walls.

> *Subject 20:* is bedridden with Parkinson's disease. Good appetite but husband is unable to cook. Would like fish in meals-on-wheels.

> *Subject 21:* is blind, giddy and only manages to cook one meal per week. The neighbour cooks three midday meals but she would probably be helped by one other delivered meal a week.

> *Subject 24:* has advanced Parkinson's disease. Son has muscular dystrophy and is violent and depressed.

> *Subject 33:* sister cooks only on Sundays. Would probably enjoy luncheon club.

> *Subject 50:* an erratic eater, self neglect.

Subject 57: is crippled with arthritis. Taken by ambulance to one day centre meal which she enjoys. Relies on home help for lunch and evening snack but extra meals-on-wheels or luncheon club meals might improve diet.

Subject 60: is a nervous woman suffering from angina and caring for husband with multiple sclerosis. He has a small appetite and this affects her eating pattern.

Subject 65: is apathetic towards food preparation. Gets hungry and wants bigger portions.

Subject 98: bereaved.

Other types of extra help recommended after study of the case histories:

Subject 6: shopping advice. *Subject 9:* more social contact (in a follow-up a year later he was happy visiting other elderly people on behalf of Portsmouth Corporation). *Subject 11:* introduction to Over 60's cookery classes (she had expressed interest in discussing recipes). *Subject 15:* persuasion to buy nourishing convenience foods. *Subject 88:* possible residential care. *Subject 12:* obviously in need of extra help but this has proved extremely difficult to give. See one part of her case history under 'Shopping list and 24 hour diet recall', page 123. In addition the case history reports rheumatoid arthritis since age of 32 (doctor feels psychological factors contributory cause of illness). Has refused community life. Mentally alert with firmly entrenched ideas about how she proposes to live. Surprised when told of her low weight (41·7 kg, height 165 cm). Takes out her frustration on the world at large. The investigator blamed for headaches, nose bleeds and a day in bed. Discarded Local Authority chiropody service because she felt she did not receive civility. Criticised her doctor, the chemist, the matron of the old people's home attached to her bungalow (matron unofficially provides a bowl of porridge each day), home help supervisor, the Government and the youth of today. Early in the week she found meals-on-wheels adequate and good, but after her 'bad turn' said that they were disgusting and those who brought them thought that they were doing you a favour.

Re-appraisal of Case Studies

In Table xx (pp. 200–6) there are a number of subjects with marks indicating 'at risk' factors who had not been picked up as being at risk merely by reading the case studies. Their case studies were therefore re-appraised. When the diet records and socio-economic questionnaires were examined along with the case studies it was found that the majority did not in fact appear to be at special nutritional risk.

Subject 1: was being supported by meals-on-wheels, day centre, neighbour and social services. Not prepared to leave her home in spite of its condition.

Subject 3: although three times 'nothing' after lunch, was managing perfectly good meals; minor wastage from meals-on-wheels.

Subject 19: was a very active 84 year old. Minor wastage from meals-on-wheels. Although three times 'nothing' after lunch it was after good meals in the morning.

Subject 42: in spite of recorded loss of weight, seemed to be eating well. Cheerful and independent.

Subject 49: was well supported by friends, ill but determined to manage.

Subject 51: family provides good meals on all but meals-on-wheels days.

Subject 54: supported by a neighbour and friend. Eats frequent good meals but has diabetic arthritis and sleeps badly.

Subject 58: seems to be eating satisfactorily in spite of recorded loss of weight.

However, on this more detailed re-appraisal the following extra recommendations would be made:

Subjects 24, 47, 80, 86, 91 and 92: extra delivered meals (subject 92 needs lunches to be provided by some source at the weekends).

Other types of help:

Subject 2: advice on more nourishment at tea-time.

Subject 13: discuss value of fruits and vegetables.

Subject 22: nutritional advice.

Subject 35: introduction to a luncheon club. Possible introduction to a cookery class for the blind.

Subject 38: introduce nourishing convenience foods. Difficult shopping situation about to be eased by a new mobile shop.

Subject 59: relied heavily on meals-on-wheels and luncheon club. Her position should be kept under review in case she needs extra help in future.

> *Subject 70:* discuss with her the loss in weight. She says she eats all she wants and as much as is good for her.

Two further subjects were assessed as needing help but this would have proved difficult to give:

> *Subject 67:* ate only five main meals per week, but her refrigerator was full with packets of frozen fish fingers, vegetables and meat; apart from other food in packets and tins, there was a box the size of a tea chest in her larder filled with tins of food of all sorts.

> *Subject 85:* weight loss at time of survey could probably be accounted for by bereavement. Since her husband's death two years previously she had lost most of her zest for life. Apathetic about cooking and eating. Shunned suggestions of visiting day centres or entering into any other activity. Indifferent to size and content of meals. (*Approximately one year later:* recovered somewhat from death of husband, stopped smoking, no marked change in diet but had gained 9·6 kg making her weight 66·8 kg, height 158 cm. High carbohydrate diet with 101 g added sugar per day. Subject needs nutritional advice and possibly now would visit a day centre or luncheon club).

CONCLUSION

To pick out those at special nutritional risk, the case studies had to be examined in conjunction with other risk factors. For some subjects, some of the 'at risk' indications could be discounted as they were reasonable for the individual's pattern of living and did not appear to be affecting that individual's nutrient intake.

These findings emphasise the point made at the beginning of this chapter: namely a group of short-cut indices or guide lines taken together, rather than any single one, is more likely to select all subjects who might be at nutritional risk. However an assessment technique would be needed for fuller recommendations.

In our survey two meals-on-wheels a week appeared to be adequate for 69% of the sample so long as they continued to be able to look after themselves, or to receive support from friends, relatives or other helpers. The other 31% might be encouraged to improve their diet by other means, i.e. for 17, extra delivered meals or luncheon club meals; for 14, cookery classes, consumption of nourishing convenience foods, and nutritional advice (which, it must be faced, at least three subjects were not prepared to accept!).

11
Identifying needs

One of the most important forms of preventive medicine for the elderly is practical advice on good nutrition. Yet when a General Practitioner is faced with an elderly patient with chronic disabilities, it is all too easy to overlook the fact that the disease may well be masking malnutrition. The patients' widely varying nutritional problems will probably not even be mentioned by them or dealt with by the Doctor.

The DHSS Survey (1979) stressed that malnutrition was not easily diagnosed. Clinical signs and laboratory findings were often, on their own, unreliable indicators of malnutrition. Such surveys emphasise the importance of social factors as well as medical factors in assessing the individuals who may be at nutritional risk. It should be remembered that many elderly may be suffering from subclinical malnutrition, and unless an underlying social cause is dealt with, marginal risk may tip into actual risk.

Although rising food and fuel prices threaten to restrict nutrient intakes, equally relevant are loneliness or social isolation, bereavement, lack of basic culinary skills, physical incapacity, poor dentition, mental confusion, drug therapy, nervous state, or embittered personality.

Where there is disinterest in food resulting in low intakes or poor choice, two types of solution can be applied to help to keep the elderly in the community:

1 the provision of food, e.g. by meals-on-wheels, luncheon clubs, day centres, and assistance with food shopping and preparation;
2 non-nutritional solutions, e.g. 'Good Neighbour' visits, walking aids, or improved dentition.

The mere provision of food does not necessarily improve food intake. Food unacceptable to the individual is likely to remain uneaten; moreover, even food delivered hot, appetising and ready to eat may be left uneaten unless the underlying social, psychological or environmental problems are tackled.

Exton-Smith (1971) itemised possible causes of nutritional deficiencies in the elderly under two headings, including social as well as medical factors:

PRIMARY	SECONDARY
Ignorance	Impaired appetite
Social isolation	Masticatory inefficiency
Physical disability	Malabsorption
Mental disturbance	Alcoholism
Iatrogenic disorder (caused	Drugs
by medical treatment)	Increased requirements
Poverty	

The DHSS Report (1979) associated the incidence of under-nutrition in the elderly with the following medical and social 'at risk' factors: living alone, no regular cooked meals, Supplementary Benefit, Social Class IV and V, low mental test score, depression, chronic bronchitis, emphysema, gastrectomy, poor dentition, difficulty in swallowing, housebound, smoking and alcoholism. In many instances the factors were inter-related, and subjects in whom four or more risk factors operated were said to be at considerable risk of malnutrition. Co-existing medical causes in this list were almost invariably present in subjects diagnosed as malnourished.

The medical assessments referred to by Exton-Smith and the DHSS cannot of course be made by a meals-on-wheels organiser. Therefore, where the assessment of the extent of need, e.g. for meals-on-wheels, home helps or other facilities, is made by the Social Services, the GP can help when making a referral by indicating the physical and mental disabilities which might directly or indirectly affect food intake.

From our survey findings, as discussed in detail in Chapter 10, the following had emerged as 'at risk' factors:

1 *Fewer than 8 main meals*, hot or cold, eaten in a week. That is, sometimes less than one main meal each day.

2 *Very little milk drunk* — less than ½ pint daily.
3 *Virtual absence of fruit and vegetables* — resulting in low intake of vitamin C.
4 *Wastage of food* — even that supplied hot and ready to eat, for instance the delivered meals-on-wheels.
5 *Long periods in the day without food.*
6 *Depression or loneliness.*
7 *Unexpected weight change* — either a significant gain or loss.
8 *Shopping difficulties.*
9 *Low income* — possibly in need of Supplementary Benefit.
10 *Indication of other factors or disabilities (including alcoholism) in the case study.*

In a number of subjects, some, if not all, of these ten factors may be the result of medical conditions.

With these factors in mind, a brief questionnaire has been devised by the Gerontology Nutrition Unit for assessing and re-assessing the need for meals-on-wheels or other services available in the area. Pilot investigations using this technique have shown that individuals can be assessed without undue hurry in less than half-an-hour. The questionnaire has been specifically designed for possible use by Local Authorities.

It was essential to devise a technique which would be cost-effective, minimise paperwork, save staff time, and to ensure that local facilities are used to the maximum.

Unqualified personnel, e.g., volunteers from amongst the ranks of the newly retired, need only brief instructions on how to ask the questions in order to identify the needs and degree of risk of each individual, to be reported back to the meals-on-wheels organiser.

Designed on small index cards, the questions are formulated for easy answering; a mere tick in the appropriate box by the interviewer will give the organiser at a glance an indication of the needs of the individual which can be used as a guide when the decisions are made and implemented. The card index system also has special advantages when reassessment is required. The one questionnaire can be used throughout the changing circumstances of the individual; from the initial referral, to possible waiting list, to transfer on to meals-on-wheels list, and for reassessment of need including temporary emergencies.

In our pilot study the types of alternative services which were available in one area investigated included: a choice of luncheon clubs, community and day centres (some with facilities for the physically handicapped), a day hospital, Darby & Joan clubs, home help service, good neighbour visits and local church facilities, shopping assistance and delivery services, cookery classes, and organisations such as Task Force and Contact. Several of these local services cost little or nothing, but we found that there was a lack of liaison, so that their existence in the area was insufficiently known. Much of the information we were initially given was out-of-date or incomplete, and we found ourselves at first recommending a non-existent luncheon club. Therefore, before our pilot assessment could proceed we had to spend several days telephoning around and visiting in order to compile a list of facilities including the names of the organisers, telephone numbers, hours of opening, cost to the consumer, and transport provided. Lists are often available at the Town Hall or Library, but unless they are both comprehensive and frequently updated (possibly by the meals-on-wheels organiser) they are frustrating, and therefore counterproductive.

Once the list is compiled, if an elderly man or woman is not considered sufficiently at risk to receive immediate meals-on-wheels, the assessment will point to the type of locally available services which could better meet their needs. Merely to put someone on a waiting list without meanwhile offering positive alternatives, however small, generally leads to frustration, despair or a feeling of 'bureaucratic neglect'.

If improved circumstances of someone already in receipt of meals-on-wheels point to the advisability of stopping or cutting down on delivered meals, the assessment shows the facilities which could be offered instead.

A clear factor which emerged from this pilot study was that it is not sufficient merely to offer alternative services, or even to provide full information about them. For successful adoption it was necessary for the original interviewer to give active encouragement, e.g. a personal introduction to the luncheon club organiser to ensure an individual welcome (particularly for those who are feeling reticent), on the first and ensuing visits.

Helpers may also need encouragement! While some clients are appreciative of the smallest thought, others may over-demand or exploit, and then backtrack or wildly misinterpret even the simplest common-sense measures. Incidentally, those who shop for some old people know how essential it is to keep the price tags or the bill — inflationary prices sometimes cause surprise or disbelief and suspicion.

Initial trials of our assessment technique have been successful, and the questionnaire cards are now available for purchase from the Gerontology Nutrition Unit.

FOLLOW-UP STUDY

In 1980 — ten years after the date of our original survey — it was learned that some of our participants were still living in Portsmouth.

We had not, in 1970, contemplated a longitudinal study. The vulnerability of the group would have meant a far larger initial sample in order to obtain a satisfactory follow-up sample. However in 1980, we were able to trace survivors (5 women, 2 men), who were active enough to participate in a follow-up study, including a full week's weighed diet survey, and a repeat of the socio-economic questionnaire.

A re-investigation was undertaken to examine possible dietary changes and trends. The validity of comparing two weekly intakes with so wide a time lapse has been upheld in other follow-up studies, and although this follow-up sample was inevitably too small to allow for statistical analysis, the DHSS survey (1979) points to the importance of appraising individual case records.

For our 1980 reassessments we were able to use the same investigators and methodology as in the 1970 survey. Six of the subjects' could participate in a repeat of the seven-day weighed dietary intake. One (Miss C.) was too frail for such an investigation; a three-day dietary recall was used instead.

To enable longitudinal comparisons to be made, the original data were recalculated with the latest food tables (Paul and Southgate, 1978) used in this 1980 study.

RESULTS

As shown in Table 9, mean daily energy intakes had not decreased except in two subjects (Mr E. aged 87 years, and Mrs G. aged 80 years). When Mr E. was first contacted to participate in the re-investigation, his meal pattern was found to be unaltered. However a few weeks later he became unwell and collapsed. During his survey week an overall decrease in food intake was reported and the beginning of loss of interest in diet was reflected in the weighed intake data. He died shortly afterwards. The lower energy intake of Mrs G. was due to a deliberate reduction in fat consumption (from 82 g to 58 g) which was not compensated for by her increased carbohydrate intake.

Table 9
Mean Daily Energy, Protein, Fat and Carbohydrate Intakes

Intake		Subjects (ages in 1980)						
		Mrs L (83 yrs)	Mr C (90 yrs)	Mrs F (85 yrs)	Mr E (87 yrs)	Mrs G (80 yrs)	Mrs H (89 yrs)	Miss C (75 yrs)
Energy	1970	1376	2331	1477	2137	1727	1802	1206
(kcals)	1980	1424	2333	1447	1597	1536	1806	1336*
Protein	1970	59	64	62	68	61	60	53
(g)	1980	43	68	54	50	55	59	51*
Fat	1970	68	104	78	80	82	77	60
(g)	1980	50	84	65	61	58	75	58*
CHO	1970	141	303	141	299	199	232	122
(g)	1980	206	348	171	224	212	237	162*

*Estimated intake from a 3-day dietary recall.

Even in such a small sample it is of interest that there was a two-fold range in energy intake, which remained ten years later. The subjects had maintained their individual levels. However, Table 9 indicates that there had been alterations in the composition of their diet.

There was an overall trend of reduction in fat consumption, with a corresponding increase in carbohydrate. In 1970, fat provided 41% of the energy intake compared with 36% in 1980. Conversely, carbohydrate intakes increased from 44% to 51%. Protein provided more than 10% of the energy intakes in all subjects (1970, average = 15%, 1980 average = 13%).

In Table 10 some marked changes are recorded in vitamin, mineral and fibre intakes. The figures in the Tables could be accounted for by:

(a) *sudden decline in health (Mr E.)*

(b) *single food items eaten in the survey week*, e.g. pig's liver in meals-on-wheels accounted for a proportion of the iron intake (Mrs F., 1980)

Egg eaten daily contributed to vitamin D (Mrs F., 1970)

Table 10
Calculated Mean Daily Dietary Nutrient Intakes

		Mrs L	Mr C	Mrs F	Mr E	Mrs G	Mrs H	Miss C
Thiamin	1970	0·7	0·9	0·7	0·9	0·9	1·3	0·9
(mg)	1980	0·7	1·0	0·9	0·6	1·1	1·2	0·9*
Riboflavin	1970	2·3	1·5	1·6	1·8	1·5	1·8	3·0
(mg)	1980	1·4	1·1	1·6	1·1	1·7	2·1	2·5*
Vit. C	1970	38	32	34	38	81	72	29
(mg)	1980	68	36	42	25	40	54	91*
Vit. D	1970	1·2	1·7	2·4	2·1	5·8	2·0	1·5
(µg)	1980	0·6	1·7	1·3	2·2	1·5	0·7	0·9*
Calcium	1970	997	1151	774	1090	843	883	613
(mg)	1980	824	963	759	759	1014	857	570*
Iron	1970	9·0	9·4	7·5	11·0	8·0	7·6	17·0
(mg)	1980	7·6	11·0	12·0	8·9	6·6	9·6	13·0*
Potassium	1970	2124	2567	2216	2352	2369	2328	1645
(mg)	1980	1939	3040	2225	2023	2109	2462	1559*
Fibre	1970	10	11	8	12	11	15	9
(g)	1980	12	19	11	9	10	22	11*

*Estimated intake from a three-day dietary recall.

Bloater eaten in one meal affected vitamin D intake (Mrs G., 1970)

Orange eaten daily contributed to vitamin C intake (Mrs G., 1970)

(c) *some deliberate changes in food choice*:
Although the subjects were adhering to their customary meal patterns they were not set in their choice of foods. At this very elderly age, four of our subjects were readily influenced to change food choice for reasons of health or convenience. The main influences were:

Hearsay — e.g.: bacon and cheese excluded because 'fatty foods should be reduced when elderly'; reduction in fat consumption because 'everyone says it's better for heart patients'; Hovis and watercress are 'good for you', but not sure of the reason.

Relatives — e.g.: wholemeal bread and bran cereals bought on daughter's advice (Mrs H., 1980).

Advertising (magazines, TV, radio) — e.g.: cider-apple vinegar and honey in water as 'an aid to fitness and slimness';

daily blackcurrant drink and (as supplements not included in the weighed diet) brewer's yeast and cod-liver-oil capsules in winter (Mrs L., 1980); Ostermilk to 'revitalise the system' during a regimen of lighter foods on Sundays; margarine used instead of butter.

Convenience — e.g.: boil-in-the-bag fish, now readily available; ready-to-eat sliced meats bought to avoid cooking. Margarine easier to spread while supported by a walking frame. Wholemeal bread replaced by white 'for freshness and moistness'.

The doctor's instructions were not always followed. The subject who had angina pectoris and thrombosis had reduced her total fat consumption and had felt it important to change from butter to margarine in spite of her doctor's assurances to the contrary. Ten years previously another subject (Mr C.) had torn up the doctor's reducing diet on the grounds that everything he liked was forbidden, and that 'at my time of life I'm not going to give up eating pleasures just to live a few weeks longer'.

Physical and Mental Disabilities

Stanton and Exton-Smith (1970) stated in their longitudinal study on elderly women, that falls in energy and nutrient intakes during the eighth decade could be accounted for by the consequences of increasing physical and mental disabilities.

The DHSS survey (1979) had noted that although some diseases may be associated with an increased energy or nutrient requirement, in general, poor health appeared to be more important than age as a cause of diminished food intake in the elderly.

In our initial survey, our seven subjects were already severely physically handicapped, and one exhibited clinical signs of depression. By the time of the follow-up study further deterioration was evident (Table 11), but we have *not* demonstrated a marked overall fall in energy and nutrient intakes for this group. Only at the point of death did Mr E's intake rapidly decline.

Discussion

It is gratifying to note that in spite of their severe physical disabilities, all of these subjects (nos 11, 25, 32, 37, 40, 79 and 90 in our original survey) had been classified in our assessment a decade ago as 'managing well and not at present in need of further support'.

Table 11
Health status of Follow-up Subjects

Subject		Physical Status
Mrs L	1970	Angina pectoris. Hyperthyroidism.
	1980	Angina pectoris. Hyperthyroidism. Hyperactivity. Bronchitis.
Mr C	1970	Obesity. Bronchial asthma.
	1980	Deterioration of eyesight and hearing. Severe bronchial asthma. Arthritis. Benign prostatic hypertrophy. Loss of weight. Frail.
Mrs F	1970	Obesity. Osteoarthritis. Fractured clavicle.
	1980	Obesity. Severe osteoarthritis. Reduced mobility.
Mr E	1970	Glaucoma. Depression.
	1980	Glaucoma (almost blind). Depression. Very frail.
Mrs G	1970	Angina pectoris. Myocardial infarction.
	1980	Angina pectoris. Myocardial infarction. Thrombosis.
Mrs H	1970	Angina pectoris.
	1980	Angina pectoris.
Miss C	1970	Mastectomy. Thyroidectomy, Arm amputation. Depression.
	1980	Continued depression.

It had been thought that one subject (no. 11) could have benefited from attending cookery classes, because of her enthusiasm for discussing recipes, although in fact she did not do so. In the intervening years she had virtually given up home cooking although she was still very health conscious.

Several of the 'at risk' factors which the DHSS (1979) had associated with undernutrition were present in the follow-up study. Thus: all 7 subjects were living alone; 4 were in receipt of supplementary benefit; 4 were in Social Class IV or V; 2 were depressed (one a clinical diagnosis and the other assessed subjectively by the investigator); 2 experienced difficulties in chewing food; 1 suffered from bronchial asthma; 5 were housebound; 1 smoked cigarettes and 2 drank alcohol (although fairly moderately). In addition, 2 were obese.

In our initial assessment, the important criterion had not been the extent of disability, but rather whether the subjects were making the most of their capabilities.

The most noticeable common factor in all subjects in our 1980 follow-up was that meal patterns had remained very similar in the intervening ten years. In spite of living alone and in deteriorating health, all subjects were keeping some interest in food and maintaining a similar style of eating; that is they continued to eat at least one main meal a day, and several small light snacks and beverages throughout the day. Meals were rarely missed, so that there were no long gaps in the day without food or drink, even when intakes were low. Miss C. was too frail to take part in the seven-day weighed dietary intake, but even she showed in her three-day dietary recall that her pattern of eating had remained unchanged, although with less home cooking.

It has been emphasised that to regard old people as random survivors of a general population is to over-simplify. They are, in fact, individuals who have special characteristics which have enabled them to outlive their contemporaries.

The seven subjects in this survey could not be regarded as the 'elderly élite' described by Stanton and Exton-Smith, (1970) and DHSS (1979), who identified a group of individuals surviving to a vigorous old age with little impairment in their health and physical capabilities, and whose nutrient intake changed little with age. In subjects who survived to the second half of the eighth decade with a *decline* in health and activity, there was an associated fall in nutrient intake (Stanton and Exton-Smith, 1970). Our own subjects had reached extreme old age *in spite of* deteriorating health and physical capabilities. Nevertheless they had maintained their energy and nutrient intakes. It is possible that mental attitude or heredity, as well as nutrition, contributed to their survival.

All, with the exception of Mr E., had outside interests and hobbies, and were well supported by relatives or friends. In their own opinion, reasons for survival included 'spiritual faith', 'a loving family and a cheerful spirit', 'retaining an interest in life', 'keeping mentally and physically active' and 'coming from a strong family'.

12
'It ain't necessarily so'

The last paragraph of Chapter 10 shows the need to look at the personalities behind the statistics and the recommendations. This we did in our case studies.

To many, the term 'meals-on-wheels recipient' conjures up the picture of an elderly woman or man who is lonely, poor, neglected by family and neighbours, shabby, ill, incontinent, deaf, housebound, living in one cold, dark, damp room, unable to shop, malnourished etc. Indeed, some of these terms apply to many of our 100 subjects, but in the words of the opera 'Porgy and Bess', 'It ain't necessarily so'.

Those who deliver meals-on-wheels know that many needy clients can still be one or more of the following: frequently visited and well cared for by family, friends and neighbours, not in need of social security, smartly dressed, without serious disabilities, living in well-kept properties, retaining their faculties, enjoying getting out to the shops, and eating well. However, in the majority of such cases in our Survey, it was largely due to the assistance of the two delivered meals that they managed to keep up this standard.

Local Authorities realise that each client has individual problems, needs and expectations. They also know that there are inevitably going to be further cut-backs in the Social Services. This makes it imperative that the remaining services go to those who need them most. This is one of the reasons why I have stressed the urgent need for simple, individual assessment for requirements of meals-on-wheels and/or other services. If there are to be cuts, or a brake on expansion, which clients have the priority? Which clients have to be provided with some alternative service if their nutritional status is to be maintained? Could such alternative services cost the Local Authority less than the cost of meals-on-wheels, or even nothing? If the answer to this question is YES, the assessment technique would pay for itself! Even if the answer to this question is NO, it may still be cheaper to expand the alternative services of luncheon clubs, day hospital, home help or sheltered housing, rather than opting to pay for even more costly years in residential homes.

The case studies of our survey played an important part in our suggested assessment technique. They showed, for instance, that where a particular factor (such as physical incapacity) is a nutritional risk for some, 'it ain't necessarily so' for others. Incidentally, information comparable to these case studies is already gathered, if not actually written down, by many meals-on-wheels organisers.

In order to mask identities, the following extracts from the case studies have been altered only in names, places and minor details. In all other respects, the original wording of the investigators has been retained.

Personalities

**** She is very shrewd, never missing a trick, always willing to accept anything that is given and being in no way reticent about asking for what she considers her right. She tried to sell me two boxes of chocolates at 25% reduction, saying they were gifts and she'd rather have the money.

**** A naturally happy person, is very uncomplaining and reminds one of a typical wartime cockney — always ready with a quip and a helping hand to neighbours. His movements are quick and he says 'If it weren't for my breathing I would be on top of the world'.

**** Mrs S. prefaced almost everything she said with 'I don't mean to criticise or grumble ... ' and proceeded to complain about most things and people. She admitted that one of the things she most enjoys with her friends is having a 'good old grumble'.

**** Aged 89, Mr J. was one of the dearest old gentlemen one could wish to meet. Although long ago retired, almost everyone at his former place of work remembered him with great affection. After the survey week he wrote to me thanking me for 'immeasurable kindness.'

**** She is now a small grey-eyed anxious looking woman. Although very bronchial she is extremely voluble, and with much coughing her words tumble out endlessly, ranging from one topic to another with no apparent connection. Whenever the attempt to steer the conversation back was made, the rebuke was always the same. 'If you wait I will tell you, but as I was just saying ...'

Attitudes to Meals-on-Wheels or Luncheon Clubs

**** He was quite certain the meals-on-wheels had saved his life, for although he knew he was losing weight, he thought it was grief and never thought of lack of food.

**** He enjoys having meals-on-wheels, nevertheless on the days when he caters for himself his diet is varied and imaginative.

**** He says he appreciates not having to make preparations on meals-on-wheels days and enjoys the contact with the WRVS ladies!

**** Although saying she appreciated meals-on-wheels, she says she always throws away all carrots when they are delivered as they are not to her liking. The Cornish pasties were also discarded and labelled 'ghastly'. Chops were a popular dish with her, but the roast beef was apparently rarely tender. Beefsteak pudding was 'delicious' but the rice pudding was 'poor'.

**** Meals-on-wheels were highly praised and thought to be of excellent value. No criticism could be found and all meals were gratefully accepted. Although normally eating very little, Mrs M. says she always eats the whole of the meal delivered because they are so good.

**** She says she does not like cooking and uses mostly tinned foods, consequently enjoying roasts and tarts when they are delivered by meals-on-wheels. She is mobile and able to go out most days to shop and walk, which she loves. She started meals-on-wheels in July 1969 after an operation on her feet when she was unable to walk.

**** Meals-on-wheels although classed as good and asked for on two more days, seemed rarely to be wholly eaten, although also stated as not being too much.

**** She is very pleased with the meals-on-wheels which for two days a week give her relief from making her own preparations and from the physical strain which this entails.

**** Mrs N. is rather apathetic about cooking and eating. She feels that she cannot be bothered to cook for herself. She is perfectly able to shop and cook if she so desired and there seems to be no valid reason for her receiving meals-on-wheels. However, it is obvious that there are times when these might be the only two cooked meals of the week. It will be some time before Mrs N. takes up any outside interests. At the moment she shuns the suggestion of visiting day centres and of entering into any other activity.

**** Mrs L. supposes that she is no longer entitled to meals-on-wheels but she hasn't said anything and hopes that they will be continued. She began to attend a luncheon club in June. It is a long walk, but she makes the effort.

**** Subject had a good appetite and enjoyed being able to cook for herself when the meals-on-wheels were not delivered. She once thought of going to a Luncheon Club, but refused when she heard the old men there were not very clean.

**** He has been encouraged to go to an old people's club but does not care for it — he prefers a group of mixed age if he must join one at all. He is appreciative of the service provided by meals-on-wheels and his criticisms were constructive, based on the fact that many foods do not keep well for long periods.

Shopping

**** She is very active in spite of suffering from a bad heart and frequent attacks of angina. With great determination she continues to do her own shopping with the aid of a trolley; as she walks she takes frequent rests sitting on garden walls on the way to and from the shops.

**** Her shopping expeditions usually begin at about four in the afternoon and since she produced soft tomatoes, a tail end of fish, scrap bacon and a pan of scrap meat boiled up each day, it could be that she tries to get things cheap. Some of the food she buys is never eaten and this is thrown out or given to her old cat. She bought a food mixer for £4 10s 0d early during the survey week and intended to make some 'nice things' but at the end of a week, it remained in its box.

**** She is extremely active for her age (84 years) and does her own shopping which she has delivered to the door. As she pointed out, she does not go to a supermarket to save a penny or two and then, at her age, have to carry a load home.

Independence

**** A neighbour does most of the shopping and often provides a delicious Sunday lunch. Subject enjoys this very much but often refuses it because neighbour will not allow her to pay.

**** A well built woman active for her age (early eighties) full of determination and very talkative. She walks to the shops most days and calls in on friends as she goes. She has a rest in the chair after lunch and suffers from periodic severe bouts of coughing when talking. She keeps her house in meticulous order and raises flowers in her conservatory. She asks her home help to move heavy furniture or reach high objects during her once weekly visit.

****   She refused all walking aids saying she must keep trying however painful to move around under her own steam.

****   Visiting members of the family all expressed wishes that Mr F. would leave his flat and live with one of them. He refuses to do so saying that he is comfortable as he is. 'I've got my fire, my television, a bite to eat and all my children come to see me and take me out — what more could I want?'

****   Eyesight is extremely poor (glaucoma). He will not accept help from the RNIB. He was approached a while ago from this source and offered a white stick, but says he refused it because he 'wasn't going to have people pushing me across the road'. He accepts meals-on-wheels under sufferance, saying that he dislikes taking money out of the ratepayers' pocket, and although it is obvious that meals on more days would be of great benefit to him, he was adamant that I reported no more wanted.

****   He is insistent that he would never go into an old people's home — he likes to be free with his 'bird' (i.e. budgerigar) and his television.

Marital Status

****   He had once been engaged to be married but she had 'oft an' married a sailor' whilst he was in hospital, and he had been disillusioned about women ever since.

****   Nearly 81 years of age but looks and acts a great deal younger. He was divorced about 19 years ago. For the last 16 years he has been living with his unmarried sister, a small frail bird-like woman who worries about his going out each evening and remarked many times that 'he doesn't act his age'.

****   She and her husband are devoted to each other and it was sometimes difficult to separate their stories, one from the other. They celebrated their golden wedding last year.

****   The subject was widowed during the First World War and had a very hard life with no pension, she took in washing to bring up three children.

****   They seem in good accord with each other and Mrs McA. shows extremely patient care and concern for him. She is distressed by the progressive nature of his illness.

****   He is completely dominated by his wife who never, never stops talking, answering all the questions put to him. He talks little, stays in bed until lunch-time, I think personally for a little peace and quiet.

Loneliness

**** Welcomed the visits from the investigator because, as she put it, she was 'a talker and missing conversation more than anything'.

**** She stated many times — as previous subjects had also — that she missed her contemporary friends who were all dead, and that she is now feeling rather out of things. She is, however, quite cheerful, and enjoyed the Survey.

**** He is an extremely proud and independent man. He visits no one, and receives no visitors. He says he used to speak sometimes to a neighbour or two, but now only has an occasional word with the warden of the flats. A home help was employed at the beginning of his tenancy, but was dismissed. The reason given was that 'the money wasn't earned, and women were not wanted around anyway'. It was during demonstrations of the preparation of one or two convenience food items that Mr D. showed a kind, generous and humorous side of his nature. He confessed to having a very stubborn streak, saying he had always been an odd one out. Obviously a very lonely gentleman, Mr D. goes to lengths to hide his true nature, presenting a hard exterior to the outside world.

**** His companion is his wireless which is provided for him by the local Association for the Blind. With this he keeps up with current events and takes a great interest in politics. He welcomes company but seldom has visits from people and appears to be very lonely.

**** She began to attend a luncheon club in June. It is a long walk, but she makes the effort. She has not made friends and feels this may be because she is not of the same religion as most of the others. She is reserved and hampered by deafness. She is very lonely. Her brother visits once a week and her daughter has come down from London twice recently to take her out. She sleeps badly.

**** Mr T. says he has no friends and, other than the casual acquaintances he meets in the square, he mixes little. Says he does not mind having no callers.

**** She feels the lack of company and her name has been on the Welfare Services list for residential accommodation for some time. She lives in hope that this will be forthcoming. She visits a few friends occasionally but entertains little and her shabby surroundings play a part in inhibiting this.

**** She lives a self-contained life. She has a sister aged 82 and a niece who live near but she rarely sees them and she says that she is much happier on her own and does not need company. She much prefers the company of her cat on whom she says she spends 15s 0d to £1 a week for food.

**** Miss R. is a very self-sufficient person. She mixes with very few people but says she is never lonely. She loves living alone, having done so all her life and jealously guards her freedom, not wanting to become involved with others. A younger sister, also living in Portsmouth, and recently widowed, has automatically assumed that Miss R. will give up her home and live with her, and this is causing her some distress because she is unwilling to agree, but is uncertain how to refuse without hurting her sister's feelings. She says she feels safe being a tenant in a Council owned property, and wishes this to continue.

**** Christmas lunch is always eaten alone, and has been for fifteen years, says Miss A. An offer of a Christmas period with other people was refused. 'I save a few pennies up and buy myself a miniature bottle of cherry brandy to have with my lunch, and I would not miss it for worlds' she says.

Outside Interests

**** She has been provided with a hearing aid but will not use it. Her sight is very poor and this prevents her from reading or writing; she does not have papers or television.

**** Mentally she is very alert and, although she has a cataract over one eye, she crochets lovely blankets from pieces of coloured wool given to her by her neighbours; she also watches television and listens to the wireless.

**** Mr C. was a man of many skills, although he described himself as having 'no natural talent'. He had taught himself, secretly, to play the mandolin, when he was well into his fifties, eventually having a ten strong mandolin–guitar group of his own. There were his pencil drawings of ships around the walls that were almost 'naval architecture' in their attention to detail. Perhaps his greatest hobby for over forty years had been motor-cycling. His knowledge of the countryside, and its associated history was like a vocal ordnance survey. Undoubtedly his most treasured possession was a 1926 motor-cycle, maintained by himself and considered to be something of a museum piece, although he was still riding it until about two years ago. For a few months at the beginning of 1969 his chest condition became better, he joined another band, and became interested in stereo recording equipment. He was convinced that once you lost interest in life you might as well be dead.

Illness

**** In recent years she has had seven fractured bones as the result of falls culminating with a fractured hip when she fell two years ago. She says she has constant pain. In spite of this she maintains her garden and paints the lower half of the outside of the house.

**** Mr D. worked for over 50 years in dockyards at home and abroad at senior foreman level. He is an intelligent, lightweight (about 7 stones) man who has never had need of a doctor since the age of 7.

**** Mrs A. is a very thin frail looking woman, who suffers from arthritis, and has some difficulty in moving about. She also has psoriasis to a very marked degree, and most of her body is covered with the characteristic lesions and white scales. Her nails have a dark brown crustaceous appearance, overlapping the ends of her fingers in a claw-like manner. She uses Betnovate cream and Arachis oil extensively on her body each day, and consequently is unable to wear any smart clothing, which would be affected by the oil. Approximately three years ago she spent three and a half months in hospital with this disease, but says the improvement obtained was negligible. She leaves a trail of white scales wherever she moves and the inconvenience of this, coupled with the difficulty of getting down the two flights of stairs from her flat to the street, have caused Mrs A. to become housebound. She is very hard of hearing and spends her time reading women's magazines and paperback novels and watching television.

**** Miss F. is 70 years old, height 5' 0'', weight 5 st 3 lbs. She has had a life punctuated with periods of severe ill-health (including tuberculosis) and long spells in hospital, so that she had only spasmodic periods of work in early life when she was in domestic service. She has suffered three strokes, has hardening of the arteries and she says that she has constant head pains. Her doctor visits her regularly. She says she cannot go further than a nearby shop for fear of falling. She never buys fresh meat or vegetables because she cannot prepare them. She frequently refers to herself as a housebound person, although this is not strictly true. She would like to eat out in a restaurant but she says that it costs too much. She has a lively mind and some firm views (some based on clearly false premises!) and she has strong political views.

**** Mrs V. is a short, slightly built woman but she does not look emaciated. She walks slowly and supports herself against the walls as she moves because she fears falling down. Most of her day seems to be spent sitting in a chair. She never goes out because she feels unsteady. Her son told the interviewer that he had tried to persuade her to go in his car, but she would not.

****   A bright-eyed, cheerful little old lady, who had been very active until fracturing the neck of her femur almost a year ago. Her only complaint nowadays was that her doctor would not allow her to go outside and she longed for a walk in the fresh air. She had also been forbidden to go upstairs but she did, saying that there always seemed to be something up there she wanted.

****   The subject had advanced Parkinson's disease and could do little for herself. A visit we made to the sea front one afternoon had been, she said, the nicest thing to happen to her in years.

****   She is a large-made, fat woman who is in constant discomfort. She has chronic ulceration of the legs which swell as each day progresses. She also has an itching skin condition and suffers from incontinence.

****   She is a woman of great charm allied with common sense — but she is feeling old and will soon have her 84th birthday. She says that she gets very tired and she perfoms her tasks in short stages. In August of this year she was removed to hospital because she was suffering from severe anaemia and protein deficiency. When admitted to hospital she weighed 6 stone 3 lbs and on discharge she weighed 6 stone 10 lbs. She denies that she had neglected her food intake.

Medication

****   She says that she has had gastric trouble since adolescence and that she has a 'folded stomach' and obstructions in her bowels which are inoperable. She claims that she avoids many foods because she finds them 'binding'. She takes regularly each day, Senokot, senna pods, 'Heath and Heather' herbs and an emulsion. She says she needs these to clear her system but that she often does not succeed.

****   Mrs C. stated that she seldom takes aperients but has the occasional raw apple which has the same effect.

****   Pills taken were thyroxine, digoxin, frusemide, Slow K, Soneryl, Multivite, Andrew's Liver Salts, Carter's Liver Pills, and as a reward for 'an interesting week' Mrs M. divulged to the interviewer her 'cure' for rheumatism, from which she had apparently suffered at one time, which was to eat a sprig of parsley every morning for two years, by which time all signs of rheumatism would have disappeared.

Dentures and Chewing

**** She refused to have the dentist call, she couldn't see any point in that and besides he might try to get her to do something about the bottom set of teeth which she never wears.

**** One lone top front tooth is revealed when she smiles, which is frequently, particularly when memories are recalled of her romantic conquests in her youth. She enjoys her meals, and the meals-on-wheels menus are liked.

**** She does not wear her dentures except on social occasions away from home.

**** She wears no top dentures, but is able to eat all foods, including toffees, with a few of her own bottom teeth which she has remaining.

**** Since her stroke she has found some difficulty in chewing various foods, but has recently been fitted with new dentures and is now managing to eat all types of food.

Living Conditions

**** The three bedroomed terraced house is clean and comfortable. The downstairs only is used as Mrs K. cannot negotiate the stairs. There is a bathroom, but no supply of hot water. All hot water is heated in a kettle on the gas. The dining room is dark, all the light being taken by a built-on greenhouse in which is an enormous grape-vine, carrying at this time approximately 60 bunches of grapes. Although virtually housebound, being only able to go out with transport, Mrs K. is fairly content.

**** She continually stressed that all her money went on the electric fire, for she knew she must keep warm. She only ever had one bar on (sitting within a few inches of it) and I did not ever find the room very warm. The room had a large window, with only very thin curtains, and two doors, one to a cold large hall and the other to a very cold scullery.

**** An ex-dockyard worker. He lives with his severely disabled second wife and old dog in a ground floor, Corporation owned flat. Everything is disorderly and very dirty and their food is eaten on their laps beside a table covered with plastic which was never cleaned during the survey week.

**** She lived for some time in a flat on the seventh floor of one of a new 17 storey block of flats in the area. She felt she was 'cut off from the world' there, being used to meeting lots of people, and was eventually transferred to a ground floor corner flat on a fairly busy road with traffic passing the door. She now sits looking out of her kitchen window and watches the traffic go by.

**** Mrs G. lives in one of a group of bungalow type flats which are clustered round a green, making a small quiet close tucked behind a row of houses situated towards the outskirts of the city. The flat consists of a kitchen, bedroom, bathroom, sitting room, and small hall, and all the rooms are furnished well and are clean and bright. Although the close appears as a small haven of peace to the visitor, Mrs G. says it is too quiet for her taste as she has only the green to look out upon. She would prefer to have traffic passing her window.

**** Minster Street is narrow with dilapidated terraced houses, built almost 100 years ago, confronting one another across the pavements. No. 14 is very tumbledown with thin walls and low ceilings. It has no bathroom, no hot running water, no inside lavatory, and lighting is by gas mantles. No electricity is laid on. The rooms upstairs are empty. A room at the front of the house is not used, and Mrs A. lives in a small back room which leads to an out-house cum kitchen. In this back room she sleeps, eats and sits for most of the day. The house is dark and very dirty.

**** Miss D. lives in a Victorian terrace house which is deep and narrow; it has three rooms downstairs with a scullery at the back and a flush lavatory outside. There is no bathroom. The front room is used as a bedroom and the upstairs is empty. It is kept spotlessly clean and is owned by Miss D. She is hoping to sell it shortly and be rehoused in an Old People's flat.

**** Another of Portsmouth's 19th century terraced properties. Damp and lacking in insulation. Very hot in summer, bitterly cold in winter. Mrs L. is a fighter for her rights, has spent time at the Rates Office and the Rent Tribunal and her landlady has given up calling and sends an agent.

**** They have been advised by their doctor to consider an old people's home but they are determined to stick together in their own home, which is a Corporation-owned, untidy, dirty flat. The subject's predominating fear is that he will die before his wife.

**** The semi-detached house in which she lives alone is owned by Mrs T. It stands on one of the wide tree-lined roads leading East out of the city, and is in a good residential area. It consists downstairs of a sitting room, dining room, kitchen and a glass covered annexe adjoining the kitchen. In the annexe, which has views of the Solent, is contained the sink and extra cupboards. Water is heated over the sink by an electric water heater. Upstairs are three bedrooms and a bathroom, with a gas water heater over the bath. All rooms are tastefully furnished and well equipped, a new investment being a colour television set.

****   Now 74 years of age and lives alone in a house in one of the areas in the city scheduled for slum clearance (by 1971). As is typical in these areas, some of the adjoining houses are already unoccupied and boarded up, and the atmosphere is one of depression. New blocks of flats are being built nearby where houses have been demolished, and Mr R. is looking forward to the time when he can be accommodated in one of the flats.

****   She was rehoused when her house was compulsorily purchased and she misses the neighbourliness of her former street.

Home Help

****   Her home help was also a great friend to her, doing far more than her two hourly paid stints. As she lived close by, she often popped in to collect the pension, and do shopping.

****   She has no domestic help but keeps tidy with the aid of a long-handled brush, dustpan on a long handle and long-handled tongs, all provided by the Welfare Department.

****   He is making a gallant but hardly successful attempt to run the small Council owned flat. He will allow no home help in the flat which is consequently extremely dirty. The kitchen is particularly so with large patches of grease on the walls, very dirty cupboards and dripping taps.

****   His wife died in 1961 and since then he has lived on his own. He keeps the house spotlessly clean and tidy; he does his own washing and ironing and manages to mend and make small articles on a Singer sewing machine. He is very proud of his house and on the days when he considered the kitchen was too untidy, as on washing days, he did not allow the interviewer to see it, but brought all the necessary food into the sitting-room to be weighed.

****   Mrs E. relies on her home help almost entirely for company and her day-to-day needs. These latter take up the whole hour that the home help spends with her and there is no time left for real cleaning.

Help from Neighbours or Friends

**** Neighbours come in and out at will, and often bring items such as a piece of fried fish as a goodwill gesture. If any item of shopping is needed urgently, Mrs H. will call to children playing in the street, and they will run an errand. She was quite unable to quote costs of foodstuffs. Many items are donated by the family. 'I buy it when I want it, if I've got the money, and if not, I go without, what is to be will be' she says.

**** She is deeply hurt that her neighbours will have little to do with her in recent years. The Rector's wife who organised the luncheon club volunteered that it was impossible to get anyone to help Miss F. because of her attitude. However two Girl Guides are visiting each Saturday to do shopping for her.

Relatives

**** Partially paralysed after two strokes, she has one son and one daughter. Her son lives within the city, and her daughter on the city boundary. Between them they visit on the four days that Mrs K. receives neither meals-on-wheels nor a day centre meal, and bring with them a lunch for their mother. They shop and garden and decorate the house, and generally care for all her needs. Mrs K. has very little power in her right hand and is unable to open tins, peel potatoes, etc. and consequently is unable to cater for herself. Her speech is only slightly affected. She has four grandsons of whom she is inordinately proud, and follows their academic progress with great enthusiasm.

**** She has been divorced many years and had worked in service all her life to support her five children, two had died as young children. She would be able to leave her three surviving children £1000 between them which she found very satisfactory after her hard life. Though they did little to support her.

**** Four sons, all of whom are married; three live in Portsmouth and the fourth a few miles away. They all visit her frequently, one or other of them at least once a day. They provide her with a cooked meal on all days except Mondays and Thursdays, when she has meals-on-wheels. She goes out in the afternoons to the local Sisterhood meetings about four times a week and has a cup to tea and meets her friends. In spite of all this she says that she is very lonely and would like to live with her daughter-in-law.

**** Mr J. is obviously trying very hard to keep things running smoothly. Mrs J's sister who lives with them goes out to work each day, and consequently Mr J. has to do a great deal of the housework as they have no home help. He takes

great care of his wife and encourages her to exercise her limbs
through walking to the shops with him and he sees that she
adheres mainly to her diabetic diet, in fact doing everything he
can to help her. He does, however, show signs of stress and
admits that the last eleven months have been a time of great
strain for him.

**** He has always lived on his own until about 18 months
ago when his brother moved in with him and they took a
slightly larger bed-sitting room. He preferred living on his
own, particularly as his brother was such a bad patient and had
had 'flu for several weeks. His brother certainly looked very
ill, but would not take the medicine prescribed by his doctor,
or eat anything, or go to hospital — he just sat by the window
(with a tea-towel on his head) groaning and moaning, and this
was beginning to get subject down. It was interesting to note
that the WRVS helpers said it was the sick brother that was
usually so cheerful and friendly.

**** The subject was widowed about nine months ago. Her
husband died of lung cancer and remained at home during his
illness. They led a stormy married life and the Police were
called on more than one occasion to deal with their disputes.
She says that she is glad he is dead and speaks bitterly, wildly
and at length about his treatment of her — but discussion led
the interviewer to the belief that it was far from one-sided.
Whatever was the situation, this woman is in a disturbed
emotional state. She is tearful at times and glad of someone to
listen to her.

**** The doctor has advised that she needs to get out far
more but she is reluctant to leave her husband.

**** Widowed 30 years ago. For the previous ten years
her husband had been a semi-invalid. He had worked in the
dockyard and on the buses. She has one son, now aged 36,
who spent 15 years in a mental hospital. He attends now as an
outpatient once a month, lives in lodgings two streets away
and calls to see her for a short while each evening and does
shopping for her at weekends. She was anxious that he and the
interviewer should not meet and refused any access over the
weekend as 'he would be there'.

Cooking and Diet(s)

**** She is very conscious of eating the right food for her
complaint, and asked me to produce a list of calories and
vitamins she had eaten during the week.

**** This is a classic case of an intelligent man who, all his
married life, had never had to undertake any household duties.

However he had applied himself to the tasks of washing, cleaning and shopping, but not cooking — with which he could not come to terms. He relied completely on the advice given to him by shopkeepers, who usually suggested a pie or pasties or cold meat. He was keen to know if his diet was adequate and how it might be improved, and was amazed to learn of products on the market that were easy to prepare by 'just a mere male'.

****   All her life she has had two biscuits, two teaspoonfuls of honey and a glass of hot water before going to bed.

****   She prepares a good meal for herself each day and has it in the evening. This is a continuation of a lifetime habit.

****   She eats nothing after 4 o'clock to ensure a good night's rest.

****   The subject cannot bring herself to lead an organised life, and she is in a continual state of meaning to clean up, but the moment she begins she feels exhausted. Her eating habits follow the same pattern, and she cooks spasmodically.

****   He is reluctant to spend on anything which he does not consider to be good value, e.g., he would not buy a cauliflower in spite of liking them so much. His late neighbour was able to buy Ovaltine and Bovril for him at reduced prices at an OAP club, but this source is lost now. However he spends 3s 0d a fortnight on bird seed for his budgerigar.

****   She did not seem short of money, though grumbled about others having things 'for free' that she had to pay for. She looks well after her diet, considering this an important facet of life.

****   Aged 81, she says she eats fairly well and doesn't go without anything, but is not interested in food. She doesn't always bother to eat at any special time, and doesn't want breakfast or supper; however her egg and milk in the morning is a regular item in her diet.

****   Although overweight, she does not wish to cut down her intake of foods, for 'eating is one of the pleasures in life'.

****   Subject cannot be bothered to cook for himself; he eats when he is hungry, either something his help has brought in, or something from the small shop over the road. Says he can quite easily manage without eating knowing he has a good feed at the weekend and his meals-on-wheels twice a week.

****   He caters completely for himself but knows little about cooking, and says his diet is the same every week. Potatoes were boiled for an hour and then left in the cooking water to cool, by which time they had disintegrated into fragments. Cabbage was given the same treatment. Milk puddings, made two or three times a week, were left uncovered on a surface, and portions spooned out each day. The remains of one seen on Monday were very mildewy. There was no knowledge of simple convenience foods.

**** Subject did not have a refrigerator, saying he thought he was a bit old to buy one now. He admitted that he now had only tinned milk, because fresh milk would not keep.

**** He likes good plain food, and his wife is a frustrated fancy cook. She says that, left to himself, he wouldn't bother about food, and he agrees 'an egg would do'.

**** She can raise and support a cup and make tea but she cannot cut food. She says she is not interested in food. She is frail in appearance and was surprised on being weighed, to find that she had lost a lot of weight.

13
... and then?

Throughout this book there has been discussion together with recommendations. In this chapter there is speculation on what could lie ahead; some of the main points are re-emphasised, with additional recommendations.

In Chapter 2 attention is drawn to a report on 2100 men and women over the age of 80 in Stockport:

> About half of the subjects did not eat a hot balanced meal every day. Old people living alone often had an inadequate diet.

Our Portsmouth survey pointed out the difficulties of assessing 'an inadequate diet'. For the individual it cannot be related to the group recommendations for nutrients, and diagnosis of subclinical malnutrition is difficult. Lack of a daily hot meal may not, in itself, lead to malnutrition, but it may be indicative of general apathy. It is therefore of paramount importance *to keep up interest in food* among the elderly so that in their total diet over the weeks they eat a wide range of foods and thus obtain a wide variety of nutrients. A number of our subjects maintained their nutrient intakes, not necessarily with a hot meal every day, but with nourishing cold food or hot snacks which were within their physical capabilities to prepare.

When rising food prices threaten food purchases, it would even be possible to have *a restricted form of subsidy by introducing a welfare foods service*. This could give a rebate on the weekly food bill from delivered foods; the system has, in the past, been used for milk purchases by pregnant and nursing mothers. The importance of the doorstep delivery of foods, especially to socially isolated old people, should not be underestimated. In many areas of the UK the milkman is often their only regular caller, and frequently helps them, or summons urgent outside help in a crisis. Thus they follow a Care Code: Observe, Enquire, Action. Many milkmen now deliver, among other foods, orange and grapefruit juice, eggs, bread, cheese, butter, margarine, ham and bacon as well as milk and yogurt. These foods could provide a simple basis, delivered to the doorstep, for nourishing meals or snacks, hot or cold. A welfare foods subsidy such as this could be restricted to the needy.

If pensions or a welfare foods service do not keep pace with *the rising cost of living*, some elderly people might be forced to turn to the cheaper carbohydrate foods or to economise unwisely on food. In *Living on an Old Age Pension* (Davies 1974), the point was made that the pension must give not only enough money for an experienced good manager to achieve adequate food purchases, but must take into account the extra expenses involved if the retirement pensioner needs some convenience foods or easy-to-cook items for comfort or emergencies. To someone who is tired, handicapped, lonely or bereaved, some slight extravagances may be the practical alternatives to not eating.

In Chapter 4, the school meals service is mentioned as one of the sources of meals-on-wheels in some areas. However, meals delivered from schools or from industrial canteens generally cease during holiday periods. Similarly, in holiday districts cooks engaged in the meals-on-wheels service might find more lucrative seasonal employment in restaurants and hotels, and thus may also restrict the provision of meals-on-wheels. In our survey we found distress caused by *the closure of meals-on-wheels* even on one day during the Bank Holiday, and it is important that an alternative source of meals should be found, e.g., local hospitals or local restaurants. The latest threat is the reorganisation of school meals which will alter the traditional type of meal served. Will this affect those meals-on-wheels which come from local schools?

With two meals-on-wheels a week, the total diet of our sample (as shown in Chapter 7) was very similar to the total diet of the elderly sample in 6 areas surveyed by the DHSS, most of whom were not receiving meals-on-wheels. However the following points must be made:

1 In Portsmouth there was a high degree of community help. This may not be available in other areas, and this book *does not* indicate that two meals-on-wheels are sufficient in all areas, and for all individuals. Instead, it makes the recommendation that *the meals-on-wheels service should be made more flexible* so that whilst individuals should ideally receive the number of delivered meals necessary and wanted, they should not, under

a blanket scheme for the whole area, receive more delivered meals than they need.

2 A more flexible service, rather than an ambitious blanket scheme for a whole area, might help to *eliminate waiting lists and to give the benefits of meals-on-wheels to a larger number of people.*

It is acknowledged that some people receive meals-on-wheels because their health is deteriorating; for these people, nutritional improvement is difficult to provide or assess. It should not be assumed that the provision of meals-on-wheels, or of extra meals-on-wheels, will automatically increase the food intake in *those who are ill or neglecting their diet.* Where there are physical and psychological difficulties which might affect food intake — as indicated in the 17% of our sample recorded in the energy section of Chapter 8 — extra remedial help was suggested as well as the provision of meals-on-wheels.

The nutrient content of the diet, both at home and that provided by institutional care, depends on wise choice of foods, menus, recipes and cookery practices. With this in mind, Chapter 8 gives suggestions for *increasing the uptake of some nutrients found especially lacking* in the total diet or the delivered meals of our subjects.

In our survey, as already mentioned, there was shown to be valuable community help in Portsmouth. Appreciation of this certainly influenced many of the 59% who expressed themselves content with two meals-on-wheels per week; although a further 21% would have liked 3 per week. There was a high degree of satisfaction with the meal, and praise for all concerned with its production and distribution. On the other hand, there was strong evidence that *the recipients valued their independence* and wanted, to the best of their physical and mental capabilities, to manage for themselves or with the help of their friends, neighbours and relatives, rather than to accept more delivered meals. One example was subject 49, whose case study read:

> *Subject 49*: Mrs H. 69 years old. Rheumatoid arthritis since her 20s. During the survey week, had 13 main meals plus milk and fruit. Keeps a large stock of emergency food, relies on others to open tins. A woman of great spirit and courage. 18 years ago a kidney was removed. Number of spells in hospital with other illnesses. Permanent invalid. Delights in recalling numerous so-called amusing incidents of her falls in the garden and

having to drag herself back into the house so that the milkman, when he came, could pick her up. She insisted that it should be recorded that she prepares her meals on days when meals-on-wheels are not delivered. Although vegetables were cut up by visitors, all other items of food she somehow manages to prepare for herself, e.g., uses a foot for kettle switch, prepares a tray of cold food for evening.

Not only should *'good neighbour' services* be encouraged, but it should also be remembered that *old people themselves can help each other.* The provision of shared meals as well as visits from the neighbour might help to persuade some listless old people to eat. However, since the time of our survey, food prices have risen so considerably that neighbours, friends and relatives may no longer be able to afford to provide meals for these elderly people as they were providing them in 1970. Even if they were to charge for them — which some were reluctant to do — the elderly recipients might not be able to afford all of the cost of a meal which, unlike meals-on-wheels, carries no subsidy.

The importance of 'good neighbour' services was apparent in Portsmouth, but the case studies frequently mentioned re-housing because this was in progress in parts of Portsmouth at the time of the survey. In re-housing the elderly it is essential to consider the effects of the break-up of a community and to enquire into the help being given by neighbours and near-by relatives. For example Subject 54 when moved into a Corporation flat, no longer received meals and shopping help from her new neighbours.

Nutritional status of the elderly is inextricably linked with non-nutritional factors. Improved social care, the diagnosis and treatment of disease, or help with a physical handicap may spectacularly improve interest in food. Conversely, provision of easy-to-eat, appetising food, is sometimes of little benefit if the person is too miserable or lonely to develop an appetite.

The outcome of our investigations was the suggestion of a simple standard 'at risk' assessment technique to review the meals-on-wheels list, and to check the needs, social and nutritional, of individual meals-on-wheels recipients, or would-be recipients. The technique of investigation described in Chapter 11 does not need the services of already hard-pressed meals-on-wheels organisers; instead, *part-time investigators* could be instructed to gather the information for subsequent assessment by the qualified authorities.

If there is no waiting list, and the Local Authority budget allows, it may sometimes be desirable to continue meals-on-wheels once the urgent need is past. However, this is not to be recommended if it keeps needy people off the meals-on-wheels list or — by increasing the list — reduces the quality of the service. *Once the urgent need for meals-on-wheels is past,* it might be more beneficial both to the individual and to the Local Authority to suggest one or more of the alternatives mentioned in Chapter 11, e.g., more help with shopping or food preparation.

We have come a long way from the first WVS meals-on-wheels described in this book: a few home-cooked meals delivered by volunteers driving a private car, or even wheeling a bicycle or pram. What have we now? There has been a marked increase in Local Authority involvement. Some meals are cooked by volunteers some by paid meals-on-wheels cooks. Some come from other sources such as schools, industrial canteens, Service establishments, luncheon clubs, hospitals, residential homes, or restaurants. In a number of areas there is reliance on ready-prepared frozen meals.

Many people feel that such *flexibility*, particularly through the continued use of volunteers, should be retained. Others suggest that there is a need to *standardise* delivered meals so that all recipients have the same type of meal and the same nourishment for the same price. Perhaps the best course would be continued flexibility and voluntary effort, but with the addition of carefully researched central advice.

Although advice on nutritional values is essential, the isolated quoting of nutritional goals such as weights of food items or grams of protein, can lead to a false sense of security.

I see as the most important, urgent nutritional goal: to *translate nutrients into popular recipes and methods,* and to *keep up the quality of the ingredients and the cooking.* Good cooking practices and an inspired choice of menu, resulting in appetising texture, flavour, aroma, colour and temperature, will do most to ensure that a wide variety of nutrients is consumed.

Where there appears to be a need for advice on improving nutrition of the individual, it is obvious that the *meal pattern of the subject needs to be studied.* In our Portsmouth survey, the main meal was eaten at midday; after this, 23% of our sample were going for long apathetic intervals without eating, i.e., not preparing a nourishing afternoon or evening snack. In other areas, where evening meals were eaten, the interest in food preparation might flag throughout the morning and afternoon. *Nutritional counselling should therefore centre on the periods of low-ebb interest, and offer ideas for easy-to-prepare, nourishing snacks or meals during those times.* It is noteworthy that all the men and women taking part in our longitudinal study (Chapter 11) had maintained their healthy interest in food, and were eating snacks or meals (even if small in size) at intervals throughout the day.

It has sometimes been suggested that in order to spread the delivery load, more meals-on-wheels could be delivered in the late afternoon or in the evening. In some areas, particularly where newly retired people have been used to evening meals, evening meals-on-wheels may be more acceptable than they would have been in Portsmouth. Whatever the time decided upon, *it is important to keep to the same time for each individual.* It was found in Portsmouth that if a meal arrived later than usual, the subject may already have taken a snack which then spoiled appetite for the delivered meal.

In investigating the number of main meals consumed per week, I used the 'protein meal' criterion of Stanton (1971) as described in Chapter 10 (p. 122). This calls for only a small serving of protein, but I would suggest that even less than the recommended '1 oz cheese' might be considered adequate in the *protein meal criterion.* Several subjects consumed only ½–¾ oz cheese (sometimes this was the weight of a wrapped portion). However with this, they had bread, sometimes salad, and generally a milk drink or milk in tea or coffee. These subjects were put in a lower 'meals' category, possibly too low, because they did not meet the standard of 1 oz cheese.

A combination of meals-on-wheels and luncheon clubs may be even more valuable than either taken separately. Luncheon club facilities, day centres or day hospitals are invaluable, particularly for those who suffer from depression or loneliness. In Portsmouth, meals-on-wheels and luncheon club meals were, in 1970, considered as alternatives one to the other. However, many elderly people are only active enough to make the the effort to visit a club once or twice a week; moreover a club may not be open every day of the week. On the other days it may still be necessary to provide a delivered meal. Incidentally, it is unfortunate that luncheon club meals are generally more expensive to buy than the meals-on-wheels in the area; thus some people may be positively discouraged by the price from venturing into company and away from the isolation at home.

The DHSS Circular 5/70 has described meals-on-wheels as 'inevitably a second-best service, since they involve an interval between cooking and service which would ordinarily be unacceptable'. However when circumstances allow, meals-on-wheels could become a better service if they were complemented by visits to a luncheon club and, possibly, *nutritional and shopping suggestions to the clients and those looking after them.*

Our elderly men and women often mentioned *shopping difficulties.* These may be caused by the introduction of supermarkets replacing the small local shops which had a delivery service. Sheldon (1948) drew attention to the physical strain of queueing. Subjects in his survey only very exceptionally used queues after 75 years of age (the ageing woman tended to give up queueing some 5 years before she had to abandon housework) and many of those studied went without delicacies in order to avoid a queue. Although in our survey 68% had others to do their shopping for them, shopping should be a social activity to be encouraged whenever possible. Some shops already provide shopping assistance, e.g., chairs, help at cash till, but such help should become more widespread, and more delivery services are needed.

In Chapter 10, the importance of *nourishing convenience foods* is stressed. Although many are nourishing, some are less so, and it is difficult to choose between them. Where technological advances influence a food product, it is essential that the nourishment it provides is considered in relation to the meal it replaces. For example, recently soups in one-serving packets have been extensively advertised — often with the older person in mind. After pouring a powder into a cup, all that needs to be done is to stir in some boiling water. This ease in preparation is ideal, but when this soup is poor in nutritional content and takes the place of a nourishing snack or meal, it adds to the risks of those who are already poorly nourished. In one popular savoury soup the first ingredient listed is sugar, and one portion supplies only 1·4 g protein.

An easy to prepare packet soup is an excellent concept; the boil-in-the-bag technique is also excellent; so is a convenience-type meal reconstituted in a heatproof container; but the importance of nutritional content must be considered, especially where advertising of these foods is directed towards an elderly audience, many of whom will opt for convenience foods because they dread dependence on other people. They may be opting for malnourishment.

Among a long list of possible secondary causes of malnutrition, Professor Exton-Smith cites drugs (Chapter 11). When assessing the nutrition of the elderly there is one aspect of drug prescription which is becoming more important in recent years: *drug-nutrient interaction*. Where intakes of nutrients are shown to be only marginally adequate, these intakes may become inadequate when certain drugs are administered.

The elderly, who are prone to diseases, are increasingly treated with drugs and indeed many of them insist on having medication. In our sample, (Chapter 9), seventeen were not taking medication, but the majority were taking several types of drug either on doctor's orders or self-prescribed.

Our concern with over-medication was endorsed by a survey on all elderly patients in a London general practice (Law and Chalmers, 1976). Overall, these patients of 75 years and over were prescribed about three times the number of drugs prescribed for the general population. About one third were taking 3 or 4 different drugs each day; one man took 10 a day, 8 of them self-prescribed. Women took twice as many drugs regularly as men. Twenty-five per cent of the drugs were self-prescribed or recommended. There was extensive hoarding of drugs. The practitioners had rarely asked to see what medicines the patients already had when prescribing. Sometimes the labels were indecipherable, or gave insufficient directions.

All of this is alarming, especially because experimental and clinical evidence suggests that the ability to metabolise and dispose of active drugs decreases progressively with age. Furthermore, the interaction of drugs and nutrition is becoming more documented (Basu, 1977; Hyams, 1981). Two aspects of this interaction are:

1 Effect of nutritional status, e.g. low vitamin C, on drug metabolism.
2 Effect of drug treatment on nutritional status by:
    (a) decreasing appetite (e.g. indomethacin).
    (b) increasing appetite (e.g. insulin, steroids, some antihistamines).
    (c) impairing absorption (e.g. tetracycline).

(d) affecting mineral and vitamin metabolism (especially thiazide diuretics, barbiturates, steroids).

Many elderly people themselves complain of lowered appetite, often attributable to drug-induced *confusion, depression and apathy* (e.g. sleeping pills); or *impairment of food flavours.* Drugs may leave 'a bad taste in the mouth' and this often leads to exessive sucking of sweets, which in turn may dull appetite, and thus affect nutrient intake.

In other words, drug-nutrient interaction may invoke a vicious circle:

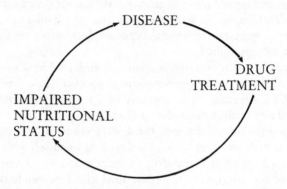

To break this circle it may be necessary to increase the intake of a nutrient (e.g. extra potassium foods as part of potassium supplementation with oral diuretics); or to decrease the dosage of a drug (e.g. when advisable, paediatric doses followed by phasing out, of digitalis).

Where possible, nutrient supplementation should be given in the form of foods. Foods are unlikely to give the side-effects which may result from large doses of nutrients in drug form; moreover they are less likely to be confused with other medication.

The lists of possible causes of nutritional deficiencies in the elderly (Chapter 11) point to the urgency for including a study of practical nutrition in medical training. It should be clear, for instance, that the diagnosis of bronchitis, stroke or a fractured femur needs to be followed not only by medical treatment, but also by an awareness of the importance of nutritional counselling.

A great deal of work remains to be done on nutrient recommendations for the elderly, because of factors such as absorption, deterioration, illness and convalescence, mobility, drugs and, perhaps foremost, adaptation. Our survey has reported survival to an advanced age, on a very wide range of nutrient intakes, including some intakes which appear to be very low. Research is needed to improve biochemical techniques of assessment of nutritional status, and to clarify the diagnosis of marginal deficiency.

SOME PRACTICAL COMMUNITY SCHEMES

When I look at the 'help for the elderly' schemes operated by the community to meet local needs, the majority of them seem to have one aspect in common: they encourage pensioners to participate, remain independent and make their own decisions.

Coincidence? Or do they merely reflect the wishes of the local elderly population? Certainly in our Portsmouth survey the right to have independence in thought and action was frequently expressed, alongside gratitude for assistance from the Welfare Services.

There are many community schemes for the elderly in different parts of the United Kingdom. Some ideas have flourished and then faded away; others have failed, but might succeed if introduced at another time or in another area. A few typical community schemes are outlined below; all reflect types of need.

Home-cooked Luncheon Club Meals

In a North London Community Centre the pensioners opted to buy, prepare and cook their own lunches at the club every Wednesday and Friday. When told that they would have to revert to the food supplied by the Social Services Department Central Kitchen, they refused on the grounds that 'the dinners from the Central Kitchen are pre-cooked, sliced and frozen. They may only need warming up, but they can't touch our hot roasts'.

Spreading Commitments with a Rota System

In another area a rota system has been introduced. The pensioners take turns in pairs, to cook the weekly club meal. On average each volunteer cooks the lunch club meal only once in two months, and so is not over-burdened.

Computer Shopping Service for the Handicapped and Housebound

In Gateshead, a computer is linking a big supermarket with display units in several day centres and sheltered home complexes. At present the units are giving up-to-date information about prices. A later possibility is the addition of a 'dial-in' facility, so that shoppers could place orders direct to the store for delivery to their homes by volunteers.

However, an Editorial in *Yours* (a monthly newspaper for older people, produced by Help the Aged) points out that this will not overcome, and indeed may encourage, isolation. The Editorial stresses the need of the majority of elderly people for the human contact provided by going down to the shops, looking at things, meeting people. The following schemes meet this need:

Self-help Shopping Project

In East Newcastle there is a community shop run by local residents, with help from Age Concern and Newcastle City Council; it is in an area with no nearby public transport and with the nearest shopping centre a mile-long trek uphill. Customers can buy everything in small quantities, down to one egg and a single slice of bacon. Because the shop is non-profit making, prices are kept low. The shop has been so successful that it has been extended to provide, in addition, an advice centre and meeting place.

Day Centre on Wheels

In Sunderland, a mobile day centre towed by a minibus, has regularly been visiting a nearby village on Tuesdays, and a large council estate on Wednesdays and Thursdays. It provides lunch and refreshments, catering for different groups of people each day from 10 am to 3 pm. A published report (from Help the Aged) says that the centre has proved itself economic and acceptable, providing companionship and recreation for some 40 frail and mildly disabled people. This type of scheme has potential in meeting local needs when there is little money to spare from statutory services.

Pensioners Helping Other Pensioners

The Civil Service Retirement Fellowship encourages their retirement pensioners to become voluntary visitors in order to give active help, advice and companionship to ex-colleagues. Some firms run similar schemes, where pensioners are given training courses on the type of practical advice which can be passed on to other pensioners.

Lunches in Village Schools

At a village school and community college near Cambridge, members of the local Old People's Community Association visit once a week for an inexpensive lunch, and recreation. They are welcomed by the older students doing community service work. In some other schools pupils studying home economics are responsible for cooking the meals fo their elderly visitors.

This meets the needs of small villages where there are no day centres or luncheon clubs, but this type of service could well be affected by cuts in school expenditure.

Independence in Meal Preparation at Home

Gas and Electricity Councils and the Disabled Living Foundation are among the organisations which provide information about the large number of aids designed to help the disabled in the kitchen and dining room, e.g. switches operated by elbow, walking stick or foot; brailled controls; easy-to-handle cutlery and kitchen gadgets. Many of these aids have stemmed from ideas or prototypes supplied by old people themselves.

Food in Long-stay Geriatric Wards

In a long-stay geriatric ward in Cornwall the menu was changed to offer the patients a choice at breakfast and supper-time. This was part of an experiment aimed to provide greater variety, less wastage, and to improve the standard of catering and nutrition without adding to costs. A number of changes were involved, such as replacing the large tea of cakes, bread, butter and jam, with an afternoon fruit round (the patients' fruit peeled and cut up). Supper which had previously been wasted as it was so close to tea-time, is now served later in order to lessen the gap between supper and breakfast time.

As a result of all the changes, food became a regular topic of conversation and pleasure, and patients who had previously been withdrawn and disinterested regained some of their dignity and individuality (Furbank, 1974).

Return from Hospital

In a Hertfordshire Geriatric Hospital, a kitchen adjoining the ward has been fitted out so that patients can practice and demonstrate their ability to prepare meals before being discharged to return home.

PRACTICAL STEPS BASED ON FINDINGS FROM THE PORTS-MOUTH SURVEY

There is a need for survey findings with nutritional information to be expressed in simple practical terms.

Small-scale Recipes

Because about 70% of the elderly in the UK live in 'one or two person households', it was considered important to communicate simple nutrition education in an acceptable form to this group. For this reason a book of small-scale and nourishing recipes was designed. The paperback *Easy Cooking for One or Two* (Davies, 1972) was based on the needs shown in our survey, and included nutritional advice centred on three simple food rules for those living on their own; storecupboard lists and recipes for the permanently or temporarily housebound; budget cooking to attempt to offset rising food prices; and food for 'non-cooks' i.e. nourishment calling for the minimum of preparation. (This can help to improve the nutritional status of the physically handicapped and also those who are generally eating nothing beyond a beverage and a biscuit after lunch.)

A companion volume *More Easy Cooking for One or Two* (Davies, 1979) included cooking for companionship, i.e. encouragement to invite a friend to share an appetising but very simply prepared meal, to overcome the widespread loneliness apparent when people eat at home alone. There is a large print edition of the first book for the semi-sighted, and the same recipes and advice have been taped on cassette, for the blind and partially-sighted at home. Many of them already use these recipes in cookery classes.

Extension of Cookery Classes to more Areas — for both Men and Women

The setting-up of more cookery classes for the over 60s, and also for pre-retirement groups, was actively encouraged by the Gerontology Nutrition Unit, both for the social and nutritional advantages.

Easy Cooking for Larger Numbers

Wastage from meals-on-wheels may point to the necessity to improve menus and/or cooking practices. There is urgent demand for more advice on cooking in quantities suitable for meals-on-wheels rounds, luncheon clubs, residential homes for the elderly, and geriatric wards, in order to improve nutrition, variety and acceptability. Moreover, the more acceptable and enjoyable the menus, the less is the likelihood of wastage of food and money.

The fundamentals of nutrition as applied to cooking practices and menu planning should be explained simply, remembering that many of the cooks who need the information are semi-skilled and untrained.

Catering and Nutrition in Residential Homes for the Elderly

A one-day symposium on catering for the elderly, including meals-on-wheels, was organised by the Gerontology Nutrition Unit (GNU) at Queen Elizabeth College in 1974. At this symposium it became evident that there was a gap in research on institutional style catering related to the elderly.

The GNU later conducted a survey in old people's residential homes, and isolated 26 'at risk' nutritional factors (Davies and Holdsworth, 1979, 1980). The outcome has been a series of one-day seminars for Matrons/Officers-in-Charge and Chefs/Cooks from these homes. Their nutritional problems were often the same as those already found in the meals-on-wheels survey e.g. long periods between cooking and consumption of vegetables.

Many cooks in residential homes are untrained, or used to institutional style catering rather than popular home-style cooking. I suggest short, intensive training courses could enable enthusiastic family cooks to undertake the small/large-scale catering and nutritional requirements of a home.

HEALTH EDUCATION

In the DHSS *Nutrition Survey of the Elderly* (1972) there was a recommendation 'That health education for and about the elderly be extended as an important preventive measure. The number of Preparation for Retirement courses should be increased, and more extensive use be made of the skills of dietitians, health visitors, and social workers.' As a result of this recommendation, cartoon slide lecture kits were produced by the Gerontology Nutrition Unit (1973–5), based on evidence of needs and interests shown by our survey.

The first four titles were:

An Emergency Food Storecupboard. Our investigators reported that many subjects had no emergency stocks of food in the house. It only needed bad weather, a temporary illness or a cancelled visit from the home help or neighbour, to leave those people housebound without the means of making a meal.

Keeping Foods Fresh without a Refrigerator. Seventy-eight per cent of our sample in 1970 did not possess a refrigerator. Our investigators were worried about the risks of food poisoning, and waste of food with poor storage conditions, particularly as old people are advised to keep their rooms warm, and often there was no cool larder. Today these worries are still valid, even though there are greater numbers of refrigerator and freezer owners among the elderly.

What is a Balanced Diet? Our investigators found many subjects worried about whether they were eating the right foods for good health.

The Need for Vitamin D and Calcium. Explains the role that these nutrients play throughout life.

Lectures to the elderly are mostly given in the crowded noisy atmosphere of Darby and Joan clubs or day centres, where the audience is not ready or willing to concentrate for long, and is far happier talking than listening. Cartoon slides were deliberately chosen to encourage them to interrupt, ask questions, relax and to identify with the situations depicted. The lectures are also given to home helps, health visitors and others, including school-children, who visit the elderly and can take the information to them in their home, together with reminder leaflets provided.

CHANGES IN FOOD CHOICE AMONG THE ELDERLY

It is often assumed that the elderly are resistant to dietary changes and will not try new foods. To test this assumption a study of food changes in 100 elderly men and women living in a town in southern England was undertaken by the Gerontology Nutrition Unit (Bilderbeck *et al* 1981). A questionnaire was designed to uncover what food changes, if any, had occurred and the reasons for the changes.

Every individual had made some alteration to food habits. The main reasons for change were health, the ease of obtaining convenience foods, the availability of familiar foods in one- or two-portion sizes, changes in family circumstances, and a desire for variety and ease of use, even if it involved an alteration in traditional cooking methods.

The study included details of change in some basic foods such as bread, breakfast cereals, milk, butter and margarine. Over half the sample had changed the type of bread used. The main reasons given for changing to brown or wholemeal bread were ones of health and taste. Health was also the main reason given by 26% who had changed to a higher fibre breakfast cereal. Alterations had been made by 38% in the type of milk consumed; 12 subjects were now using dried milk for reasons of health, including weight reduction.

Usage of butter or margarine had been altered by 43%; butter was mainly selected for its taste, margarine mainly for health but also taste and price.

In summary, the data from this study indicated that a high proportion of these elderly men and women were making dietary changes, especially where they had been informed (or misinformed) that the change could improve health. Such a study endorses the importance of health education for the elderly.

RECOMMENDATIONS FOR FUTURE RESEARCH

Acceptability of Frozen Meals-on-Wheels

Local Authorities are increasingly turning to commercially frozen meals as a cost-effective means of producing meals-on-wheels. More research is needed into the acceptability of such meals to an elderly population, remembering that these may be delivered frequently, and that over a long period they may be the only hot meals consumed. The nutrient content needs to be assessed *at the time of consumption*; also, with rising food and fuel costs, comparative costs and portion control need to be monitored.

Other freezing techniques, such as blast freezing of home-style cooking, should be similarly investigated for use in meals-on-wheels.

Alternative Type of Delivered Meal for Subsequent Days

In both urban and rural areas the transport and delivery of meals-on-wheels may be the most difficult problem. It might be useful if more than one meal could be delivered at the same time. More research is needed into the type of meal which could be delivered on one day for safe consumption on subsequent days. This could also help to make the meals-on-wheels service more flexible, i.e. some subjects could receive two meals-on-wheels per week and, on the same delivery round, others could be provided with four or more.

The Catering Research Unit at the University of Leeds has been developing a number of alternative methods for providing meals to the housebound elderly. These include:

1 Individual frozen meals delivered in the frozen state for reheating when required.
2 Pouched long-life food — meals which have a shelf life of up to one year without refrigeration.

3 Raw ingredient packing, providing the fresh food ready prepared, with simple cooking instructions.

They too, recognise that advanced technology in itself is not
enough. The resultant meal must be appetising.

Meals for Special Diets and Ethnic Groups

In Portsmouth there was little call for special diet meals-on-wheels,
and the Local Authority had no special arrangements. Only 5
subjects were on a special diet ordered by the GP, and 4 were on
self-imposed diets.

In some areas kosher and other special diet meals-on-wheels are
being provided. There is also a growing need for more regional and
ethnic meals-on-wheels and lunch club recipes. This is an area for
recipe research, and costing for feasibility of special diet meals.

Nutrient Interaction

We have referred to the growing interest in drug-nutrient interaction. In addition there needs to be monitoring in the elderly, of the
effect of altered nutrient intakes, e.g. what are the effects of
'megadoses' of vitamins or high-fibre diets on other nutrients?

Longitudinal Surveys : Pre- and Post-retirement

Retirement from work can bring about drastic changes in family
and business relationships, and leisure interests. The quality of life
may change, especially where there is unhappiness, loneliness or
apathy. Such non-nutritional socio-economic or psychological factors can markedly affect dietary status.

The present limited number of studies of the elderly, with the
emphasis particularly on the over-70s and over-80s, are concentrat-
ing on the older survivors more than on the 'young elderly'.
However, nutritional problems and restrictive food habits, which
often become exaggerated with advancing age, could be more easily
corrected at this younger pre-retirement age.

The Gerontology Nutrition Unit has designed a longitudinal
study, including nutritional counselling in the implementation of
pre-retirement advice. Our investigation is monitoring nutrients of
special concern in relation to altered circumstances prior to, and
during, retirement. The aim is to postpone for as long as possible
the more expensive crisis interventions of welfare meals, domiciliary care and hospitalisation. A preventive approach could protect
those who otherwise might be at risk.

To return to the theme of the first chapter of this book, the criterion we should be looking for is not just the number of years, but — for each individual — the quality of those years; not only survival, but a healthier survival; not to be regarded merely as 'the elderly' but, with Biblical respect, as one of the Elders.

References

Age Concern (1973). *Shopping for Food*. National Old People's Welfare Council.

Age Concern (1978). *The Elderly — their welfare and their use of the Social Services*. Research Unit Profile, Volume 5.

Basu, T.K. (1977). *J. Hum. Nutr.* **31**, 449–458.

Bender, A.E. and Davies, L. (1968). *Brit. J. Geriatric Practice*, **5**, (4), 331.

Bhaskar Rao, D. and Kataria, M.S. (1967). Camberwell Nutritional Survey, *Medical Officer*, 21st April 1967, 207.

Bilderbeck, N., Holdsworth, M.D., Purves, R. and Davies, L. (1981). *J. Hum. Nutr.* (in press).

Bransby, E.R. and Osborne, B. (1953). *Brit. J. Nutr.*, **7**, 160.

British Medical Association (1950). *Report of the Committee on Nutrition*, London.

Brockington, F. and Lempert, S.M. (1966). In: *The Social Needs of the Over-Eighties* (The Stockport Survey of the Aged). Manchester, Manchester University Press.

Comfort, A. (1977). In: *A Good Old Age*, London, Mitchell Beazley Ltd.

Corless, D., Beer, M., Boucher, B.J., Gupta, S.P. and Cohen R.D. (1975). *Lancet*, **1**, 1404.

Dall, J.L.C. and Gardiner, H.S. (1971). *Geront. Clin.*, **13**, 119.

Dall, J.L.C., Paulose, S. and Fergusson, J.A. (1971). *Geront. Clin.*, **13**, 114.

Davidson, S., Passmore, R., Brock, J.F. and Truswell, A.S. (1979). *Human Nutrition and Dietetics*, Edinburgh and London, Churchill-Livingstone.

Davies, L. (1972). *Easy Cooking for One or Two*, Harmondsworth, Penguin Handbooks (also Magna Print Books).

Davies, L. (1974). *Nutrition*, xxviii No.1, 25–30.

Davies, L. (1979). *More Easy Cooking for One or Two*, Harmondsworth, Penguin Handbooks.

Davies, L. (1981). Nutrition and malnutrition in the elderly. In: *Geriatrics for Everyday Practice* (Ed. von Hahn, H.P. and Andrews, J.S.), Basel, Karger.

Davies, L., Hastrop, K. and Bender, A.E. *Modern Geriatrics* (1973a) 3, 7, 385; (1973b) 3, 7, 390; (1973c) 3, 9, 482; (1974a) 4, 5, 220; (1974b) 4, 11, 468; (1975) 5, 5, 12.

Davies, L. and Holdsworth, M.D. (1979). *J. Hum. Nutr.*, **33**, 165–169.

Davies, L. and Holdsworth, M.D. (1980). *J. Am. Diet. Ass.* 76, **3**, 264–269.

Davies, L., Holdsworth, M.D. and Purves, R. (1980) *Social Work Service*, **24**, 10–13.

DHSS (1969). Recommended Intakes of Nutrients for the United Kingdom. *Rep. Publ. Hlth. Med. Subj*, **No. 120**, London, HMSO.

DHSS (1969). Food Composition Tables (Personal Communication).

DHSS (1970). Circular 5/70. *Organisation of Meals-on-Wheels.*

DHSS (1972). A Nutrition Survey of the Elderly, *Report on Health and Social Subjects,* **No. 3,** London. HMSO.

DHSS (1973). *Meals-on-Wheels Short Term Study,* P.A. Management Consultants Ltd.

DHSS (1975). Catering in Homes for Elderly People.

DHSS (1979) Recommended Daily Amounts of Food Energy and Nutrients for groups of people in the UK., *Rep. Hlth. Soc. Subj.,* **No. 15,** London, HMSO

DHSS (1979). Nutrition and Health in Old Age, *Rep. Hlth. Soc. Subj.,* **No. 16,** London, HMSO.

DHSS (1979). *Personal Social Services, Local Authority Statistics.*

Durnin, J.V.G.A., Lonergan, M.E., Wheatcroft, J.J., Norgan, N.G., Macleod, C.C., Macfarlan, M.A.S. and Chambers, M. (1966). The Energy Expenditure and Food Intake of Middle-aged and Elderly Farmers. *Proc. VII Int. Congr. Nutr.,* Hamburg.

Durnin, J.V.G.A. and Passmore, R. (1967). In: *Energy, Work and Leisure,* London, Heinemann.

Evans, E. and Stock, A.L. (1971). *Nutr. Metabol.,* **13,** 21.

Evans, E. and Stock, A.L. (1972). *Nutrition,* **xxvi,** 87.

Exton-Smith, A.N. (1970). *Nutrition,* **xxiv,** 218.

Exton-Smith, A.N. (1971). Nutrition of the elderly, *Br. J. Hosp. Med.* **5,** 639–45.

Exton-Smith, A.N., Millard, P.H., Payne, P.R. and Wheeler, E. (1969). *Lancet,* **2,** 1154.

Exton-Smith, A.N. and Scott, D.L., Eds (1968). *Vitamins in the Elderly.* Bristol, John Wright.

Exton-Smith, A.N. and Stanton, B.R. (1965). *Report of an Investigation into the Dietary of Elderly Women Living Alone.* King Edward's Hospital Fund for London.

Exton-Smith, A.N., Stanton, B.R. and Windsor, A.C.M. (1972). *Nutrition of Housebound Old People,* King Edward's Hospital Fund for London.

FAO/WHO (1973). Energy and Protein Requirements, *WHO Tech. Rep. Ser.* **No. 522,** Geneva.

Fowlie, H.C., Cohen, C. and Anand, P. (1963). *Geront. Clin.,* **5,** 215.

Fox, R.H., MacGibbon, R., Davies, L. and Woodward, P.M. (1973). *Br. Med. J.,* **i,** 21–4

Furbank, M. (1974). *Nursing Times,* **70,** 1501.

Gerontology Nutrition Unit (1973–5). (a) *The Need for an Emergency Food Store Cupboard;* (b) *Keeping foods fresh without a refrigerator;* (c) *What is a balanced diet?* (d) *Vitamin D and calcium.* (Nutrition Education Cartoon Slide Kits). Queen Elizabeth College, London, W.8.

Harris, A.I. (1959). *Meals-on-Wheels Services,* Central Office of Information, **S.S. 288,** London, HMSO.

Harris, A.I. (1968). *Social Welfare for the Elderly,* Vols. 1 and 2, **S.S. 366,** London, HMSO.

Harris, J., Mapson, L.W. and Wang, Y.L. (1942). *Biochem. J.*, **36**, 183.
Heath, M.R. (1972). *Brit. Dent. J.*, **132**, 145.
Hobson, W. and Pemberton, J. (1955). In: *A Medical, Social and Dietary Study of Elderly People Living at Home in Sheffield*, London, Butterworth.
Hutchison, R. and Mottram, V.H. (1948). In: *Food and the Principles of Dietetics*, 10th Edition. London, Edward Arnold.
Hyams, D.E. (1981). Drugs in the Elderly. In: *Geriatrics for Everyday Practice* (Ed. von Hahn and Andrews), Basel, Karger.
Jefferys, M. (1976). In: *Care of the Elderly* (Ed. A.N. Exton-Smith and J.G. Evans), London, Academic Press 1977.
Judge, T.G. (1968). *Geront. Clin.*, **10**, 102.
Judge, T.G. and Cowan, N.R. (1971). *Geront. Clin.*, **13**, 221.
Judge, T.G. and Macleod, C.C. (1968). *Proc. of the 5th Europ. Meet. of Clin. Geront.*, Brussels, p.295.
King Edward's Hospital Fund for London (1965). *Notes on Diets for Old People in Homes and Institutions.*
Law, R. and Chalmers, C. (1976). *Brit. Med. J.*, **1**, 565.
Leaf, A. (Jan. 1973). *National Geographic*, 93–113.
Leeming, J.T., Webster, S.P.G. and Dymock, J.W. (1973). In: *Textbook of Geriatric Medicine and Gerontology* (Ed. J.C. Brockenhurst), p.321, Edinburgh, Churchill Livingstone.
Lempert, S.M. (1960). *Public Health*, **74** (10), 382.
Local Authority reports:
  Bedfordshire (1978). Social Services Department, *The Meals Service in Bedfordshire.*
  Camden (1980). Social Services Department. *Nutritional Survey on Camden's Meals-on-Wheels Service and Luncheon Clubs.*
  Harrow (1977). Department of Social Services, *Meals-on-Wheels Survey.*
  Havering (1974). Social Services Department, Research Report No. 2. *An Examination of the Meals-on-Wheels Service in Havering, and Proposals for its Development.*
  Hillingdon (1977). Domiciliary Services Evaluation, Part IV. *The Meals-on-Wheels Service.*
  Kingston-upon-Thames (1974). Social Services Department, *Meals-on-Wheels Study.*
  Nottingham (1972). Confidential Report, Social Services Committee, *Report of a Survey on Meals-on-Wheels.*
  Scottish Health Service Studies No. 35 (1976). *Meal Services for the Elderly in Scotland*, Scottish Home and Health Department, Edinburgh.
  South Glamorgan County Council (1976). *Survey on Main Meals in Day Centres and Meals-on-Wheels.*
  Worcestershire (1973). Local Government Operational Research Unit, Report No. C.134. *Meals-on-Wheels in Worcestershire.*
Lonergan, M.E. (1971). *Nutrition*, **xxv**, 30–6.
Macleod, C.C., Judge, T.G. and Caird, F.I. (1974). Nutrition of the elderly at home. *Age and Ageing*, **3**, 158–66 and 209–20.

McCance, R.A. and Widdowson, E.M. (1960). The Composition of Foods, *Special Report Series* **No. 297**. Medical Research Council, London, HMSO.
Tables based on the Food Composition Tables of McCance and Widdowson, 1960. Macleod, C.C., McLennan, W.J. and Caird, F.I. (unpublished).
McGandy, R.B., Barrows, C.H.Jr., Spanias, A., Meredith, A., Stone, J.L. and Norris, A.H. (1966). *J. Gerontol.*, **21**, 581.
McKenzie, J.C. (1975). In: *The Concept of Poverty* (Ed. Peter Townsend), London, Heinemann.
Maddison, J. (1963). *How to keep the Old Folks Young*, County Council of Middlesex publication.
Marr, J.W., Heady, J.A. and Morris, J.N. (1961). In: *Proceedings of the 3rd International Congress of Dietetics*, p.85. London, Newman Books.
Milne, J.S., Lonergan, M.E., Williamson, J., Moore, F.M.L., McMaster, R. and Percy, N. (1971). *Br. Med. J.*, **iv**, 383-6.
Min. of Ag., Fish. and Food (1973). *Household Food Consumption and Expenditure: 1970 and 1971*, A Report of the National Food Survey Committee, London, HMSO.
National Research Council (1974). *Recommended Dietary Allowances: A Report of the Food and Nutrition Board*. 8th revised edition. National Academy of Sciences and National Research Council Publication, Washington, D.C.
Paul, A. and Southgate, D.A.T. (1978) *McCance and Widdowson's The Composition of Foods*. London, HMSO.
Platt, B.S., Eddy, T.P. and Pellet, P.L. (1963). *Food in Hospitals*, London, Oxford University Press.
Platt, B.S., Gray, P.G., Parr, E., Baines, A.H.J., Clayton, S., Hobson, L.A., Hollingsworth, D.F., Berry, W.T.C. and Washington, E. (1964). *Br. J. Nutr.*, **18**, 413.
Population Figures.   Sources: Office of Population Censuses and Surveys; General Register Office (Scotland); General Register Office (Northern Ireland).
Schmidt, M.D. (1975). *Gerontologist*, **15**, (6), 544.
Sheldon, J.H. (1948). In: *The Social Medicine of Old Age*. London, Oxford University Press.
Shock, N.W. (1972). In: *Nutrition in Old Age*, Symposium of the Swedish Nutrition Foundation.
Southgate, D.A.T. (1972). Dunn Nutrition Laboratory, Cambridge (personal communication).
Stanton, B.R. (1971). *Meals for the Elderly*. King Edward's Hospital Fund for London.
Stanton, B.R. and Exton-Smith, A.N. (1970). *A Longitudinal Study of the Dietary of Elderly Women*. King Edward's Hospital Fund for London.
Taylor, G. (1968). In: *Vitamins in the Elderly* (Eds. A.N. Exton-Smith and D.L. Scott), p.51. Bristol, John Wright & Sons Ltd.
Thompson, F. In: *Lark Rise to Candleford*, London, Oxford University Press (1938); London, Penguin (1973).

Townsend, P. (1963). In: *The Family Life of Old People*, p. 43, Harmonds-worth, Pelican.

Townsend, P. and Wedderburn, D. (1965). *The Aged in the Welfare State*, London, G. Bell & Sons.

Vir, S.C. and Love, A.H.G. (1979). *Am. J. Clin. Nutr.*, **32**, 193.

Walker, S. (1974). *Health and Social Services Journal*, May 25th, 1974.

Watkin, D.M. (1968a and b). In: *Vitamins in the Elderly* (Eds. A.N. Exton-Smith and D.L. Scott), p.81 and p.75. Bristol, John Wright & Sons Ltd.

White House Conference on Aging (1971). *Nutrition — Background and Issues*, (Eds. E.N. Todhunter and D.M. Watkin).

Wilsher, P. (1970). In: *Pound in Your Pocket 1870–1970*. London, Cassell.

Women's Royal Voluntary Service (1975). *Meals-on-Wheels and Luncheon Clubs Handbook* (to be revised).

Appendix A

Table i
Weekly Nutrient Intakes (mean and range)

Nutrients	Men 65–74 years (10 subjects)	75 years and over (16 subjects)	Women 65–74 years (24 subjects)	75 years and over (50 subjects)
Energy (kcals)	2160	2150	1600	1750
Range	1450–3000	1550–2660	1000–2340	1210–2640
(MJ)	9·0	9·0	6·7	7·3
Range	6·1–12·5	6·5–11·1	4·2–9·8	5·1–11·0
Total Protein (g)	65	68	56	55
Range	53–81	47–103	28–82	34–76
Animal Protein (g)	44	46	41	37
Range	37–59	23–87	17–68	22–55
Protein Energy %	12·0	12·6	14·0	12·3
Range	10·1–14·7	10·3–20·8	10·1–21·2	9·1–16·8
Fat Energy %	38·5	38·0	39·9	39·5
Range	27·3–44·5	30·5–47·4	33·3–46·9	31·0–55·2
Carbohydrate (g)	273	270	191	216
Range	169–359	156–393	101–314	99–390
Added Sugar (g)	105	87	53	66
Range	52–198	13–147	6–112	5–160
Calcium (mg)	880	940	820	750
Range	563–1278	568–2152	392–1525	443–1245
Iron (mg)	11·2	11·5	9·9	8·4
Range	7·5–14·6	7·9–15·6	7·1–15·9	4·8–11·9
Thiamin (mg)	0·9	0·9	0·8	0·8
Range	0·6–1·2	0·5–1·3	0·4–1·2	0·4–1·2
Riboflavin (mg)	1·5	1·6	1·3	1·2
Range	1·0–2·0	0·8–3·3	0·7–2·3	0·7–1·7
Niacin (mg)	11·6	12·4	9·9	9·2
Range	7·8–16·7	8·9–18·9	5·7–14·1	5·7–13·7
Pyridoxine (mg)	1·2	1·2	1·0	0·9
Range	0·9–1·7	0·8–2·1	0·7–1·2	0·5–1·6
Folic Acid (μg)	66	55	51	40
Range	35–162	31–102	14–149	14–73

Nutrients	Men 65–74 years (10 subjects)	75 years and over (16 subjects)	Women 65–74 years (24 subjects)	75 years and over (50 subjects)
Ascorbic Acid (mg)	43	44	47	37
Range	19–77	12–107	10–140	16–127
Vitamin D (μg)	1·9	2·1	1·8	1·4
Range	0·8–4·5	0·4–6·1	0·3–8·7	0·3–4·8
Vitamin A (μg retinol equiv.)	1000	1130	950	750
Range	460–2180	660–1870	370–2520	310–1750
Sodium (g)	2·5	2·5	1·9	1·8
Range	1·4–3·6	1·2–4·1	0·9–2·8	1·0–3·5
Potassium (g).	2·4	2·6	2·1	2·0
Range	1·8–3·3	1·8–4·1	1·1–4·1	1·3–2·6
Magnesium (mg)	250	260	200	180
Range	160–400	150–440	100–430	120–260
Cobalamin (B_{12}) (μg)	14	15	13	10
Range	7–27	7–34	7–21	5–21

Table ii
Intake of Nutrients According to Age (100 subjects)

Nutrient	65–69 years (15 subjects)	70–74 years (19 subjects)	75–79 years (25 subjects)	80–84 years (33 subjects)	85+ years (8 subjects)
Calories	1800	1730	1790	1900	1790
Protein (g)	63	56	55	61	50
Protein % kcal	14·0	12·9	12·3	12·8	11·2
Fat (g)	80	77	79	84	75
Fat % kcal	38	38	38	38	36
Carbohydrate (g)	217	214	222	232	239
Carbohydrate % kcal	48	49	50	49	53
Calcium (mg)	880	800	800	820	680
Calcium per 1000 kcal	490	460	450	430	380
Iron (mg)	10·8	9·8	9·1	9·2	9·0
Iron per 1000 kcal	6·0	5·7	5·1	4·8	5·0
Vitamin C (mg)	47	44	37	37	51
Thiamin (mg)	0·80	0·80	0·79	0·86	0·76
Thiamin per 1000 kcal	0·44	0·46	0·44	0·45	0·42

Table iii

Dietary Intakes of Older and Younger Subjects Compared

Nutrients	Mean for 100 subjects	65–79 years Mean for 59 subjects	80 + years Mean for 41 subjects	Recommended Daily Intakes (RDI)
Calories	1820	1770	1880	1900–2350
Protein (g)	58	57	59	48–59
Protein % calories	12·7	12·9	12·5	approx. 10
Fat (g)	80	79	83	—
Carbohydrate (g)	225	218	234	—
Calcium (mg)	810	820	790	500
Iron (mg)	9·6	9·8	9·2	10
Ascorbic Acid (mg)	41	42	39	30
Vitamin D (µg)	1·7	1·7	1·7	2·5
Folate (µg)	48	49	46	—
Thiamin (mg)	0·8	0·8	0·8	0·8
Riboflavin (mg)	1·3	1·3	1·3	1·3–1·7
Vitamin A (µg retinol equiv.)	880	900	840	750

Table iv

Comparison of Average Energy and Nutrient Intakes in Two Surveys

	Men				Women			
	QEC[1] Age 65–74 years	DHSS[2] Age 65–74 years	QEC Age 75 and over	DHSS Age 75 and over	QEC Age 65–74 years	DHSS Age 65–74 years	QEC Age 75 and over	DHSS Age 75 and over
Energy (kcal)	2160	2340	2150	2100	1600	1790	1750	1630
(MJ)	9·0	9·8	9·0	8·8	6·7	7·5	7·3	6·8
% RDI*	92	104	102	100	78	87	92	86
Total Protein (g)	65	75	68	68	56	59	55	54
% RDI	109	126	129	128	111	116	113	112
Calcium (mg)	880	910	940	880	820	800	750	730
% RDI	175	182	188	177	163	159	150	145
Iron (mg)	11·2	12·2	11·5	10·9	9·9	9·4	8·4	8·5
% RDI	112	120	115	110	99	90	84	90
Thiamin (mg)	0·9	1·1	0·9	0·9	0·8	0·8	0·8	0·7
% RDI	100	122	113	113	100	100	113	100
Riboflavin (mg)	1·5	1·6	1·6	1·4	1·3	1·3	1·2	1·1
% RDI	88	94	94	82	100	100	92	85
Vitamin D (µg)	1·9	3·3	2·1	2·7	1·8	2·3	1·4	2·1
% RDI	76	132	84	108	72	92	56	84
Vitamin C (mg)	43	43	44	38	47	40	37	34
% RDI	143	143	147	127	157	133	123	113
Vitamin A (µg retinol equiv.)	1000	1140	1130	1100	950	1030	750	890
% RDI	133	151	150	146	127	137	100	118

Two surveys (1) Gerontology Nutrition Unit, Queen Elizabeth College. (QEC)—present report.
(2) Department of Health and Social Security (DHSS, 1972), p.21 (figures rounded off).
*Recommended intakes of nutrients for the UK (Department of Health and Social Security, 1969). Recommended Daily Intake = RDI.

Table v

Intake of Ascorbic Acid According to Age

		Age Range			
		65–69	70–74	75–79	80+
This Study	No. of subjects	15	19	23	43
	Mean intake, mg/day	43	41	34	35
		70–73	74–77	78+	
Exton-Smith &	No. of subjects	24	17	19	
Stanton (1965)	Mean intake, mg/day	42	36	29	

Table vi

Comparison of Analysed and Calculated Ascorbic Acid Content of
Frequently Served Vegetables

Food	No. of samples analysed	Ascorbic Acid Content (mg/100g)		
		Analysed		Food tables
		Mean	Range	
Mashed potato	38	1	0·4–2·6	10
Roast potato	22	6	0·9–13·8	14
Cabbage and greens	24	11	0·4–40·9	20
Canned mixed vegetables	9	< 1	0·2–0·7	5
Canned carrots	13	1	0·1–1·6	2
Fresh carrots	19	< 1	0·1–0·6	4

Table vii
Main Sources of Ascorbic Acid in Total Diet During Survey Week

	No. of subjects	Mean weight eaten per day (g)	Mean daily ascorbic acid supplied (calculated figure) (mg)
Fruit			
Blackcurrants	1	49	69
Blackcurrant syrup	3	24	62
Oranges	20	44	22
Strawberries	6	23	14
Gooseberries	3	25	10
Fresh grapefruit	3	21	8
Blackberries	1	24	5
Bananas	35	30	3
Vegetables			
Potatoes	99	87	9
Tomatoes	54	28	6
Brussels sprouts	9	17	5
Cabbage or greens	70	21	4
Cauliflower	22	16	3
Swedes	22	19	3

Table viii
Potassium Content of Foods: Analysis and Tables Figures*

Food	No. of samples	Laboratory analysis mg/100 g		McCance & Widdowson food tables mg/100 g
		mean	*range*	
Canned Peas	10	161	126–188	201
Fresh carrots	10	170	120–265	87
Canned carrots	8	164	105–228	84
Spring greens and cabbage	15	131	94–189	108
Mashed or creamed potatoes	18	303	118–315	302
Roast potatoes	10	462	211–565	745
Canned rhubarb	5	199	142–243	327
Canned stewed apple	4	85	52–142	95
Canned prunes	5	283	233–374	432
Lamb chop	4	251	209–293	230
Roast beef	5	314	273–326	290
Steamed cod	2	333	327–346	360
Rice pudding/ semolina	9	170	86–190	162
Custard	25	170	121–242	160

*The variation in the Laboratory Analysis and the Food Tables figures for fruit and vegetables could be due in part to the use of fertilisers, but the most usual cause of wide disagreement in potassium figures lies in the moisture content of the samples. This would especially be expected for fruits and vegetables, even more so when they have been canned or stewed (Southgate, 1972; personal communication).

Table ix
Potassium Intake Related to Depression

Mean daily potassium intake	No. of subjects depressed	No. of subjects not depressed
< 50 mmol (2 g)	20	12
> 50 mmol (2 g)	15	53

7 subjects with very low dietary potassium intake i.e. less than 30 mmol (1·5 g) per day:
  Mean daily energy intake = 1200 kcal (5·0 MJ), which was 800 kcal (3·3 MJ) below their RDI.
The other 93 subjects:
  Mean daily energy intake = 1850 kcal (7·7 MJ), which was only 150 kcal (0·6 MJ) below their RDI.
Therefore a low dietary energy intake seemed to be associated with a low potassium intake.

35 subjects were considered to be depressed:
  Mean daily energy intake = 1600 kcal (6·6 MJ), which was 390 kcal (1·6 MJ) below their RDI.
  Mean potassium intake = 49 mmol (1·9 g), range 31–105 mmol (1·2–4·1 g).
The other 65 subjects, not considered to be depressed:
  Mean daily energy intake = 1920 kcal (8·0 MJ), which was only 100 kcal (0·4 MJ) below their RDI.
  Mean potassium intake = 59 mmol (2·3 g), range 28–105 mmol (1·1–4·1 g).

Therefore depression seemed to be associated with a low energy intake combined with a low potassium intake.

Table x
Daily Energy Intake*

Energy intake		Men MJ	kcal	Women MJ	kcal
Recommended daily intake					
55 up to 75 years		9·8	2350	8·6	2050
75 and over		8·8	2100	8·0	1900
Intake of survey subjects					
Whole week	mean	9·1	2170	7·1	1690
	range		1450–3190		1000–2640
Meals-on wheels days	mean	9·5	2265	7·5	1800
	range		1280–3440		820–2700
Delivered meal	mean	3·2	760	3·2	760
	range		190–1170		190–1170
Other weekdays	mean	9·0	2160	7·0	1660
	range		1560–3210		930–2760
Weekends	mean	8·8	2100	6·8	1630
	range		1220–3020		800–2750

*Seventy-four subjects ate more on meals-on-wheels days. (20 were eating an extra 400–800 kcal.) However, the remaining twenty-six subjects ate *less* on days when meals-on-wheels were delivered.

Table xi
Number of meals-on-wheels (m/w) Wanted as Affected by the Subject's Opinion of the Meal

No. of m/w wanted	Opinion of Meals Excel-lent	Good	Ade-quate	Poor	Very bad	No. of subjects
2	13	26	17	3	0	59
3	6	11	4	0	0	21
4	1	5	2	0	1	9
5	2	0	2	0	0	4
6	0	0	0	0	0	0
7	0	2	3	2	0	7
TOTAL	22	44	28	5	1	100

Table xii
Number of meals-on-wheels Wanted as Affected by the Length of Time They Have Been Supplied

No. of m/w wanted	Receiving m/w for less than 1 month	Receiving m/w for 1–5 months	Receiving m/w for 6–11 months	Receiving m/w for 1 year–1 yr 11 months	Receiving m/w for 2 years or more	No. of subjects
2	0	3	9	12	35	59
3	0	1	2	4	14	21
4	1	0	1	1	6	9
5	0	0	1	0	3	4
6	0	0	0	0	0	0
7	0	0	1	3	3	7
TOTAL	1	4	14	20	61	100

Table xiii
Number of meals-on-wheels Wanted as Affected by the
Subject's Ability to Prepare Own Meal

No. of m/w wanted	Main meal usually prepared by themselves	Main meal usually prepared by others	No. of subjects
2	48	11	59
3	15	6	21
4	9	0	9
5	3	1	4
6	0	0	0
7	6	1	7
TOTAL	81	19	100

Table xiv
Number of meals-on-wheels Wanted as Affected by
Mobility of Subject

No. of m/w wanted	Fully mobile and competent	Limited mobility	Helpless	No. of subjects
2	12	46	1	59
3	6	15	0	21
4	3	6	0	9
5	1	3	0	4
6	0	0	0	0
7	1	6	0	7
TOTAL	23	76	1	100

Table xv

Number of Meals-on-Wheels Wanted as Affected by the Composition of the Subject's Household

No. of m/w wanted	Living alone	Living only with spouse	Living with spouse and other relatives	Living with other relatives but no spouse	Boarding	Other	No. of subjects
2	46	6	1	5	0	1	59
3	17	1	0	2	1	0	21
4	7	1	0	0	0	1	9
5	2	1	0	1	0	0	4
6	0	0	0	0	0	0	0
7	6	1	0	0	0	0	7
TOTAL	78	10	1	8	1	2	100

Table xvi

Number of Meals-on-Wheels Wanted as Affected by Visits from Relatives

No. of m/w wanted	Visited by relatives							No. of subjects
	Never	Daily	Weekly	Monthly	3-monthly	Half-yearly	Yearly	
2	7	13	19	8	2	6	4	59
3	2	1	9	2	2	1	4	21
4	0	3	1	2	1	2	0	9
5	1	0	0	0	1	0	1	4
6	0	0	0	0	0	0	0	0
7	2	1	1	1	0	1	1	7
TOTAL	12	18	31	13	6	10	10	100

Table xvii

Number of Meals-on-Wheels Wanted as Affected by Visits from Friends and Neighbours

No. of m/w wanted	Visited						No. of subjects
	Never	Daily	Weekly	Monthly	3-monthly	Half-yearly	
2	11	26	14	6	1	1	59
3	3	11	5	1	1	0	21
4	0	4	3	1	0	1	9
5	1	2	1	0	0	0	4
6	0	0	0	0	0	0	0
7	1	1	4	0	1	0	7
TOTAL	16	44	27	8	3	2	100

Table xviii
Nutrient Intake of Females 65–74 Years
Bottom Category 'Meals' Compared to Top Category

Subj. No.	(kcal)	Energy (MJ)	Total protein (g)	Protein/ Energy %	Fat/ Energy %	Potassium (mmol/ 1000 kcal)	Potassium (mmol)	Vit. C (mg)	Iron (mg)	CHO (g)	CHO/ Energy %
'Meals' Criterion: *Bottom category* (8 or fewer protein meals per week) 5 subjects											
12	1053	4·41	39	14·2	40·6	28	31	15	7·5	123	45·2
60	999	4·18	28	10·9	33·3	36	36	31	6·1	144	55·7
68	1820	7·62	61	13·0	39·6	28	54	38	10·0	222	47·4
69	1885	7·89	54	11·0	34·1	26	51	32	11·9	268	54·9
86	1506	6·30	51	13·2	39·9	30	59	26	8·5	181	46·9
MEAN	1473	6·08	46	12·5	37·5	30	46	28	8·8	188	50·0
'Meals' Criterion: *Top category* (14 or more protein meals per week) 6 subjects											
4	1645	6·89	45	11·1	39·5	30	54	33	8·0	203	49·4
50	1652	6·91	61	14·4	41·1	28	49	40	9·3	188	44·5
53	1290	5·40	52	15·7	45·3	38	51	53	8·7	129	39·0
54	2011	8·42	90	17·5	42·3	51	105	53	12·3	208	40·3
66	1430	5·98	55	15·1	38·7	33	51	42	10·7	170	46·3
75	1332	5·57	72	21·2	45·4	41	56	82	9·6	113	33·4
MEAN	1560	6·53	62	15·8	42·1	38	61	50	9·8	169	42·2

Table xix

Relationship Between 'Meals' and Data from Questionnaires, Diet Records, Case Histories and Nutrient Intakes
(No. of subjects)

'Meals' Category	No. of Subj.	Daily Milk Intake (pints)			Mental Assessment		Shopping		M/W Wastage		After Lunch		Supplementary Benefit	
		Under 1/2	1/2–3/4	1 or over	Lonely & depressed	Not depressed	Others	Self	Wastage	No wastage	'Nothing'	Eating	Yes	No
Top (14 'meals' or over)	28	7	15	6	13	15	15	13	9	19	0	25	12	16
Middle (9–13 'meals')	45	13	23	9	12	33	30	15	19	26	12	26	26	19
Bottom (8 'meals' or less)	27	9	13	5	10	17	23	4	15	12	11	16	17	10

'Meals' refer to the protein meal criterion described in Chapter 10 i.e. a meal containing not less than 1 oz of meat, 2 oz of fish, 1 oz of cheese or 1 egg.

Table xix indicates the number of 'meals' eaten in the survey week.

Vitamin C: the computer data showed calculated, not analysed figures. As stated in Chapter 10, largely due to delays between cooking and consumption, true vitamin C intakes on days when meals-on-wheels were delivered were generally lower than the

per day is classed as a poor intake, even though a calculated value as high as 29 mg might normally be considered adequate.

Iron: although the RDI for elderly men and women is 10 mg, we found the mean intake for the women in our survey (as in the DHSS 1972 survey) to be lower than this. The mean for the poorest group — elderly women over 75 years — was 8·4 mg. We therefore took a figure of below 8 mg iron as an indication of a poor intake.

Potassium: as stated in Chapter 8, most diets provide from 50–150 mmol potassium per day. We therefore took a figure of

Table xix (continued)
Daily Nutrient Intakes – From Computer Data and 'Meal' Pattern
(No. of subjects)

Category	Vitamin C (mg)			Iron (mg)		Potassium (mmol)			Potassium/1000 kcal (mmol)			Carbohydrate (g)			CHO/Energy %		Total Protein (g)		
	0-29	30-59	60+	<8	8+	<50	50-69	70+	<25	25-35	>35	300+	200-299	<200	48+	<48	<48	48-60	>60
Top (14 'meals' or over)	8	15	5	3	25	5	18	5	4	17	7	5	8	15	6	22	2	10	16
Middle (9-13 'meals')	15	22	8	13	32	16	26	3	6	32	7	8	22	15	25	20	6	22	17
Bottom (8 'meals' or less)	14	9	4	12	15	10	16	1	4	15	8	3	15	9	22	5	10	11	6

indicate a middle category. Translated into figures of potassium/1000 kcal, these gave: poor category, under 25 mmol; middle category, 25–35 mmol.

Carbohydrate: a high carbohydrate diet was taken to be approximately 30 g or more per day. As a CHO/Energy % of 48 was the mean for the elderly in our survey, the poorest category, i.e. high

carbohydrate diet, was taken to be above 48%. This generally included foods containing a high proportion of sugar.

Protein: at the time of the survey, the lowest DHSS RDI for protein was for women over 75 years: 48 g (10% of the total energy requirement). Our poorest category for all our subjects was therefore taken to be below 48 g.

Table xx
'Score Sheet' of Possible 'At Risk' Factors for Each Subject
(* = acknowledged risk factor; X = non-proven risk factor; Ø = below group RDI)

Subj. No.	'Meals'	Milk	Vit. C	M/W Wastage	'Nothing' After Lunch days/week	Depression	Weight Change ±4kg	Non-Shopper	Suppl. Benefit	Recommendation
1	*		Ø		*2			X.		OK
2	*		Ø	*	*7	*		X	X	Advice
3			Ø	*	*3			X		OK
4		*						X		
5										
6	*			*	*3	*	*−8 kg	X		Shopping advice
7								X		
8					*2			X		
9					*2					Social contact
10		*						X		
11									X	Cookery classes
12	*	*	Ø	*	*7	*		X	X	Difficult
13	*	*	Ø	*				X	X	More fruit and veg.
14	*		Ø					X	X	extra m/w
15	*	*	Ø		*6			X		Convenience food
16			Ø	*		*		X	X	m/w and L/Club

Table xx (continued)

Subj. No.	'Meals'	Milk	Vit. C	M/W Wastage	'Nothing' After Lunch	Depression	Weight Change ± 4 kg	Non-Shopper	Suppl. Benefit	Recommendation
17								X		
18								X		
19			Ø	*	* 3				X	OK 3 times 'nothing' was after good meals
20	*	*	Ø	*				X	X	extra m/w
21	*	*					* −4 kg	X	X	extra m/w
22	*	*	Ø				* −6·3 kg	X	X	Was overweight
23	*	*						X		
24	*	*	Ø	*		*	* −10·8 kg	X	X	Ill extra m/w
25				*					X	
26					* 2			X	X	
27				*		*			X	
28		*						X	X	
29									X	
30	*	*		*						
31			Ø	*					X	

Table xx (continued)

Subj. No.	'Meals'	Milk	Vit. C	M/W Wastage	'Nothing' After Lunch	Depression	Weight Change ± 4 kg	Non-Shopper	Suppl. Benefit	Recommendation
32										
33		*						X		L/Club
34								X		
35			Ø	*		*		X		L/Club – Classes (blind)
36		*	Ø					X		
37						*				
38			Ø	*		*	* −5.3 kg		X	Convenience foods, mobile shop
39		*				*				
40						*		X		
41		*			* 2					
42							* −4.4 kg			OK
43	*	*						X	X	
44			Ø	*				X	X	
45	'	*						X	X	

Table xx (continued)

Subj. No.	'Meals'	Milk	Vit. C	M/W Wastage	'Nothing' After Lunch	Depression	Weight Change ± 4 kg	Non-Shopper	Suppl. Benefit	Recommendation
46								X	X	
47		*	Ø	*	* 5			X	X	extra m/w
48			Ø	*		*				
49							* −10·8 kg	X		OK but ill
50	*			*		*			X	m/w or L/Club
51	*			*	* 2	*		X	X	OK
52									X	
53								X		
54						*	* −12·6 kg	X	X	OK but ill
55					* 3			X		
56		*						X		
57			Ø		* 2	*		X	X	L/Club or m/w
58							* −4·4 kg		X	OK
59			Ø		* 3	*				Watch for future
60	*	*		*	* 3	*			X	extra m/w
61				*		*		X		

Table xx (continued)

Subj. No.	'Meals'	Milk	Vit. C	M/W Wastage	'Nothing' After Lunch	Depression	Weight Change ± 4 kg	Non-Shopper	Suppl. Benefit	Recommendation
62				*		*		X	X	
63			Ø					X	X	
64				*				X		
65			Ø		* 3	*		X	X	m/w (larger portions – and more m/w)
66		*				*				
67	*			*		*		X	X	Difficult
68	*							X	X	
69	*							X	X	
70	*		Ø		* 7		* −9·6 kg	X	X	Discuss loss of weight
71		*						X		
72	*	*	Ø	*		*		X		
73								X	X	
74	*			*						
75				*					X	

Table xx (continued)

Subj. No.	'Meals'	Milk	Vit. C	M/W Wastage	'Nothing' After Lunch	Depression	Weight Change ±4 kg	Non-Shopper	Suppl. Benefit	Recommendation
76	*	*						X	X	
77			Ø			*			X	
78			Ø	*		*			X	
79				*		*			X	
80		*	Ø	*		*		X	X	extra m/w
81			Ø						X	
82				*				X		
83		*		*				X	X	OK
84								X	X	
85			Ø			*	* −9.6 kg	X	X	Difficult
86	*		Ø	*		*			X	extra m/w
87	*			*						
88	*		Ø	*				X	X	Residential care
89	*		Ø	*				X	X	
90									X	
91	*		Ø	*	* 5	*		X		extra m/w

Table xx (continued)

Subj. No.	'Meals'	Milk	Vit. C	M/W Wastage	'Nothing' After Lunch	Depression	Weight Change ± 4 kg	Non-Shopper	Suppl. Benefit	Recommendation
92	*		Ø		*7	*		X		m/w Extra help needed weekend
93			Ø					X	X	
94				*				X	X	
95		*		*		*		X		
96			Ø					X	X	
97		*		*	*3			X	X	
98	*			*	*3	*		X		L/Club
99				*						
100						*		X	X	

Appendix B

THE QUESTIONNAIRES

GERIATRIC NUTRITION UNIT
QUEEN ELIZABETH COLLEGE

PORTSMOUTH
1970

NUTRITION SURVEY OF THE
MEALS ON WHEELS SERVICE

Name.... MR E.   No 37 ....

Address.... PORTSMOUTH ....

....

....

....

Interviewer.... 2 ....

Area.... 1 ....

NUTRITION SURVEY OF THE MEALS-ON-WHEELS SERVICE FOR THE ELDERLY

Instructions to investigators.

In filling in the responses, please circle the appropriate code.

Area No..../.......

Investigator No...²......

Subject No....3.7........

QUESTIONS NOT TO BE CODED

If you had anything to eat or drink yesterday, will you tell me what kind of things you had.

BEFORE OR ON RISING?

BREAKFAST   2 cups of tea   2 slices bread and butter
            milk   and marmalade
            Sugar
            1 boiled egg   (1½ tsp Sugar in tea)

MID-MORNING   Brown ale

MID-DAY   Roast Lamb
          Greens, potatoes
          Bread and butter
          (No drink)

MID-AFTERNOON   —

EVENING   Bread, butter and cheese
          1 piece cake
          2 cups tea

BEFORE RETIRING OR IN BED

          —

Is this your normal pattern   Yes/~~No~~..............
   If not, what are the principal ways in which it varies.

What is your normal meal pattern at weekends.   As above

Do the amounts you eat vary very much from day to day.
                    ~~Yes~~/No ....

If yes, in what ways do they vary.

About how much of the following foods do you buy each week

	How much	If little or none bought – reason	Like more of (tick items)
Bread	2 Large Loaves – Stale, thrown away (Estimate over ½ loaf)		
	3 1/4 lb Cake		
Butter	½ lb 'Just over a week'		
Margarine	Never used		
Cheese	8oz		
Eggs	6		
Milk	7 pts		
Fruit	Fresh fruit not eaten. (Only concession – a few plums during season)		
Vegetables	1 tin peaches or pears		
	2 lb potatoes		
	1 lb cabbage		
Cereals	Porridge oats. Unable to estimate how long 1 pkt lasts		
	4-6 oz tapioca		
Meat	¼ lb ham (no bacon used)		
	1 ¼ lb lamb (7s 6d. Excess after 3 meals thrown away)		
Fish	None used		
Sweets	¼ lb		
Sugar	1 lb		
Alcohol	2-3 pts usually		
Tobacco	40-50 cigarettes a week		
Biscuits	½ lb		
Canned foods other than above categories			

ARE THERE ANY FOODS YOU POSITIVELY AVOID AND WHY?

FOODS	REASONS FOR NOT EATING
Any hard foods ie apples, hard biscuts Cornflakes	Chewing difficulty Very few own teeth - no dentures

WHAT ARE YOUR FAVOURITE FOODS?

Roast Leef and Yorkshire pudding
Good Cheese
Bath Chaps

What kind of cooking facilities have you?

No means of cooking	0
Ring or hot plate only	1
Gas cooker	2
Electric cooker	③
Solid fuel cooker	4
Others — state	5

Have you a refrigerator?

No	⓪
Yes	1

Sample page from weighed diet record

Date ...... 22 . 6 . 1970 ......   Day of week ...... Monday ......

Time of consumption	Food or Drink (one item per line) Description		Net weight consumed oz.	Net weight consumed decimals	Code number			For office use
7.0	Bread		2	67	0	2	2	
	Butter		0	33	4	3	6	
	Marmalade		1	00	1	5	5	
	Egg (boiled)		2	00	4	4	5	
	Milk		3	33	4	5	6	
	Sugar		0	67	1	6	1	
	Tea							
12.0	Espagnole steak	⎫	5	67	3	1	4	
	Creamed Potato		5	00	1	8	6	
	Mixed vegetables	MEALS ON WHEELS	2	00	2	5	3	
	Cherry Sponge		2	50	0	9	3	
	Custard	⎭	4	67	0	7	4	
3.0	Roses Chocolates (2 with soft filling)		0	67	1	7	2	
5.0	Bread		2	67	0	2	2	
	Butter		0	33	4	8	6	
	Cheese (Cheddar)		1	50	4	7	5	
	Cake (fruit)		1	67	0	5	6	
	Milk		3	33	4	5	6	
	Sugar		0	83	1	6	1	
	Tea							
9.0	Biscuit (Digestive)		0	50	0	4	3	
	Coffee (camp)		0	33	5	4	1	
	Milk		1	67	4	5	6	
	Sugar		0	33	1	6	1	

NUTRITION SURVEY OF THE MEALS-ON-WHEELS SERVICE FOR THE ELDERLY

Instructions to investigators.

In filling in the responses, please circle the appropriate code

Subject No.	1
	37

Area No.	2
	1

Investigator No.	3
	2

How much does each meal cost you?

Under		1/-	4
			0
1/-	-	1/5	1
1/6	-	1/11	2
2/-	-	2/5	3
2/6	-	2/11	④
3/- and over			5

What is the subsidy? (answer from records)

	5
Up to 5d	⓪
6d - 11d	1
1/- - 1/5	2
1/6 - 1/11	3
2/- - 2/5	4
2/6 and over	5

How often do you get them?

	6
1 day per week	0
2 days per week	①
3 days per week	2
4 days per week	3
5 days per week	3
6 days per week	5
7 days per week	6

How long have you been having them?

(Subject's answer)

	7
Less than 1 month	0
1 month - 5 months	1
6 months - 11 months	2
1 year - 1 year 11 months	3
2 years and more	(4)

How long have you been having them?

(correct answer from records)

	8
Less than 1 month	0
1 month - 5 months	1
6 months - 11 months	2
1 year - 1 year 11 months	3
2 years and more	(4)

Who first suggested you should have them?

	9
Health visitors	0
Welfare services	1
Own doctor	2
Home help	3
W.R.V.S	4
Voluntary Social Services	5
Hospital	6
Queen's Nurse	7
Others (state category) Neighbour (See case history)	(8)

Why? (answer from records)

	10
Living alone	0
Recent bereavement	1
De-hospitalisation	2
Illness	3
Incapacity through injury	4
Bedridden	5
Housebound	6
Not known (Subject states living alone)	(7)

What is the reason now?

(answer from subject)	11
Living alone	⓪
Recent bereavement	1
De-hospitalisation	2
Illness	3
Incapacity through injury	4
Bedridden	5
Housebound	6
No obvious reason	7

Would you like to have Meals-on-Wheels more often than you do?

If yes on how many more days per week?	12
No (See case history)	⓪
1 day	1
2 days	2
3 days	3
4 days	4
5 days	5
6 days	6

What sort of meals are they?

	13
Excellent	0
Good	1
Adequate	②
Poor	3
Very bad	4

Which type of main dish do you most enjoy?

	14
No preference	0
Roast dinner	1
Pies and puddings	2
Stews	③
Fish	4

Which type of dessert do you most enjoy?

	15
No preference	0
Milk Pudding	1
Sponge type pudding	2
Stewed fruit	3
Pastry tarts	④

What are your reactions to amounts of different types of food supplied?

	Meat	Potatoes	2nd. Veg.	Gravy	Dessert	Custard	Other	Other
	16	17	18	19	20	21	22	22A
Receive too little	0	0	0	0	0	⓪	0	0
Receive enough	①	①	①	①	①	1	①	①
Receive too much	2	2	2	2	2	2	2	2

At what time are the meals delivered? *11·45 – 12·00 Am*

At what time do you eat them? *Delivery time*

Lapse of time between above

	23
Up to ½ hr.	⓪
Over ½ hr. but less than 1 hr.	1
1 – 2 hrs.	2
More than 2 hrs.	3
Part kept to next day	4

Do you re-heat the meal?

	24
No	⓪
In oven	1
Direct on hot plate of cooker	2
Over pan of hot water	3
Other (state)	4

NUTRITION SURVEY OF THE MEALS-ON-WHEELS SERVICE FOR THE
ELDERLY

Instructions to investigators.

In filling in the responses, please circle the appropriate code.

Subject No....37.........

Area No......!..........

Investigator No....2......

Sex	25
Female	0
Male	①

Age	26
65 - 69	0
70 - 74	1
75 - 79	②
80 - 84	3
85 and over	4

Marital Status	27
Single	⓪
Married	1
Widowed/divorced/separated - within last 6 months	2
- 6 months - 1 year 11 months	3
- 2 years - 9 year 11 months	4
- 10 years or more	5
Cohabiting - investigators opinion	6

Have you any children living within five miles of your home?	28
No	⓪
Yes	1

Age of spouse if living	29
Single subjects	⓪
No living spouse	1
Living uncertain	2
Under 65	3
65 - 69	4
70 - 74	5
75 - 79	6
80 - 85	7
86 and over	8

numbers 30–32 inclusive were not used in this schedule

Retirement of subject	33
Not retired	0
Within past 2 years	1
2 - 4 years 11 months	2
5 - 9 years 11 months	3
10 - 14 years 11 months	④
15 - 19 years 11 months	5
20 years or more	6
Never worked	7

Retirement of spouse	34
Single subjects	⓪
No living spouse	1
Living uncertain	2
Not retired	3
Within past 2 years	4
2 - 4 years 11 months	5
5 - 9 years 11 months	6
10 - 14 years 11 months	7
15 - 19 years 11 months	8
20 years or more	9

Household	35
Living alone	⓪
With spouse only	1
With spouse and other relatives	2
Without spouse and with other relatives	3
Boarding with people other than relatives and paying for meals and room	4
Other	5
Cohabiting - investigators opinion	6

Who usually does most of the housework?	36
Yourself	⓪
Others:	1

(Please tick categories shown below as appropriate)

Spouse
Relatives
Neighbours
Voluntary helpers
Home helps
Privately employed helpers

How often do you <u>receive</u> visits from

People / Frequency	Relatives	Friends & Neighbours	L. Auth. Officers	Vol. Helpers	Employed Help	Doctor & Medical Auxiliaries
Frequency	37	38	39	40	41	42
Never	⓪	⓪	⓪	⓪	⓪	⓪
Daily	1	1	1	1	1	1
Weekly	2	2	2	2	2	2
Monthly	3	3	3	3	3	3
3 Monthly	4	4	4	4	4	4
½ Yearly	5	5	5	5	5	5
Yearly	6	6	6	6	6	6

How often do you <u>pay</u> visits to

People / Frequency	Clubs	Relatives	Friends & Neighbours	Doctor & Medical Auxiliaries
Frequency	43	44	45	46
Never	⓪	⓪	⓪	0
Daily	1	1	1	1
Weekly	2	2	2	2
Monthly	3	3	3	3
3 Monthly	4	4	4	4
½ Yearly	5	5	5	⑤
Yearly	6	6	6	6

Do you have meals away from home?

Place / Frequency	Club	Restaurant	Friends & Relatives	Other
	47	48	49	50
Never	⓪	⓪	⓪	⓪
1 Day per week	1	1	1	1
2 Days per week	2	2	2	2
3 Days per week	3	3	3	3
4 Days per week	4	4	4	4
5 Days per week	5	5	5	5
Fortnightly	6	6	6	6
Monthly	7	7	7	7

How long have you been having them?

Place / Frequency	Club	Restaurant	Friends & Relatives	Other
	51	52	53	54
Not having them	⓪	⓪	⓪	⓪
1 Month	1	1	1	1
2 Months	2	2	2	2
6 Months	3	3	3	3
1 Year	4	4	4	4
More than 1 year	5	5	5	5

What do they cost?

Place Cost per meal	Club	Restaurant	Friends & Relatives	Other
	55	56	57	58
Not having them	⓪	⓪	⓪	⓪
Nothing	1	1	1	1
Up to 1/11	2	2	2	2
2/- to 2/11	3	3	3	3
3/- to 3/11	4	4	4	4
4/- to 4/11	5	5	5	5
5/- and over	6	6	6	6

What travelling is involved?

Place Travel	Club	Restaurant	Friends & Relatives	Other
	59	60	61	62
Non travellers	⓪	⓪	⓪	⓪
On foot	1	1	1	1
Own car	2	2	2	2
Public Trans.	3	3	3	3
Organised free trans.	4	4	4	4
Private paid Hire	5	5	5	5

<u>Who usually prepares your main meal at home on days when Meals-on-Wheels are not delivered?</u>	63
Yourself	(0)
Others:	1

    (Please tick categories shown below as appropriate)

      Spouse
      Relatives
      Neighbours
      Voluntary helpers
      Home helps
      Privately employed helpers

<u>Who does most of the shopping?</u>	64
Yourself	(0)
Others:	1

    (Please tick categories shown below as appropriate)

      Spouse
      Relatives
      Neighbours
      Voluntary helpers
      Home helps
      Privately employed helpers

<u>Cost of Foodstuffs</u>

Money spent on food bought for home consumption by subject only.	65
Up to 19/11	0
£1 - £1. 9.11	1
£1.10.0 - £1.19.11	(2)
£2. 0.0 - £2. 9.11	3
£2.10.0 - £2.19.11	4
£3. 0.0 and over	5

Do you keep any pets and how much is spent weekly on their food?
(this answer to include domestic animals and wild birds)

	66
No	⓪
Up to 11d	1
1/- - 1/11	2
2/- - 4/11	3
5/- - 9/11	4
10/- and over	5

Are you on a special diet?

	67
No	⓪
Recommended by doctor	1
Self imposed	2

Is it?

	68
Not on diet	⓪
Low fat	1
Low protein	2
Low salt	3
Low calories	4
Soft diet	5
Diabetic - date diagnosed	6
Others - please state	7

How long have you been on this diet?

	68A
Not on diet	⓪
Less than 1 year	1
1 yr. - 4 yrs. 11 months	2
5 yr. - 9 yrs. 11 months	3
10 yrs. and more	4

Do you have a time limit for your last drink of the day?

	68B
No	⓪
Yes	1

<u>Do you take any of the following</u>?

	69
None	0
Aperients	①
Tablets and Medicines	2
Health Foods	3
Aperient & Tablets & Medicine	4
Aperient & Health Foods	5
Tablets or Medicine & Health Foods	6
All three	7

<u>Do you receive a Supplementary Pension</u>?

	70
No	⓪
Yes	1

<u>INTERVIEWER'S GENERAL ASSESSMENT</u>

Into which of the following categories does the subject appear to fall (ring only one in each case)

Competence: Mental	71
Fully alert	⓪
adequate	1
confused	2

Physical	72
Fully mobile and competent	⓪
limited	1
helpless	2

Overall dependency	73
independent	⓪
partially dependent on others	1
wholly dependent on others	2

Index